fondue

sweet & savory recipes for
gathering around the table

recipes   **Bob & Coleen Simmons**
photographs   **Alex Farnum**

weldon**owen**

7   fondue for the modern table

9   cheese fondues

39   oil fondues

55   broth fondues

69   sweet fondues

88   homemade dippers

92   sauces, accompaniments & stocks

98   basic techniques

104   glossary

109   index

112   acknowledgments

contents

fondue for the modern table

Nowadays, many of us no longer take the time to gather together around the dining table. But fondue promises to change that. An iconic party dish of days gone by, fondue has recently staged a comeback, and busy cooks are discovering that this time-honored communal dish is an easy, fun way to reconnect with family and friends.

Cheese fondue has been eaten in Switzerland for centuries, but it wasn't until the 1960s and 1970s that it became a popular party dish in the United States. The traditional oil fondues of France and broth-based meat and seafood hot pots of Asia arrived on American tables not long after. Like many of our favorite dishes, these communal pots have humble origins, often sustaining peasant families through hard times. Today, they are viewed as creative, festive ways to entertain.

Included in this book are recipes for some of the best-known fondues and hot pots, like Classic Swiss Fondue (page 13), Beef Fondue with Creamy Horseradish Sauce (page 53), Shabu-Shabu (page 62), and Bittersweet Chocolate Fondue (page 73). Other recipes are inspired by flavors borrowed from kitchens around the world, like Manchego

Fondue with Piquillo Peppers, Toasted Garlic & Paprika (page 26), Marinated Ahi Fondue with Wasabi Dipping Sauce (page 45), and Mexican Chocolate Fondue with Orange Essence (page 80).

With the proper equipment and the highest-quality ingredients, fondues can be among the easiest and most successful dishes to cook for weekday suppers or company dinners, and you'll find tips on choosing both in the following chapters. Also, preparing your own dippers will add a special touch to your meals. Turn to pages 88 to 91 to discover fast, tasty recipes for homemade Tortilla Chips, Grilled Apples, Polenta Cubes, Churros, Sugar Twists, Caramel Corn Clusters, and more. And no matter which fondues and dippers you serve, your communal-pot meals are guaranteed to delight everyone at the table.

about cheese fondues 10

classic swiss fondue 13

queso fundido 14

fontina fondue with truffle oil 17

edam fondue with bacon & smothered onions 18

pepper jack fondue with roasted garlic 19

parmesan & artichoke dip fondue 20

blue cheese fondue with port-glazed shallots 23

normandy-style fondue 24

cream cheese & crabmeat fondue 25

manchego fondue with piquillo peppers & toasted garlic 26

smoked salmon fondue with cream cheese & dill 29

french onion soup fondue 30

southwestern layered fondue 31

brie fondue with mushrooms & herbs 32

cheddar & ale fondue 35

provolone fondue with sun-dried tomato pesto 36

cheese fondues

about cheese fondues

Centuries ago, the Swiss discovered that the cheeses they made and stored in warmer months hardened over time, making them good candidates for melting and eating with chunks of dried bread during winter. Today, that classic combination has expanded to include a wide variety of imported and domestic cheeses and wines and myriad dippers.

equipment

You can use almost any type of fondue pot to serve a cheese fondue. Traditionally, it is made in a heavy, wide earthenware pot called a caquelon, which retains heat well, resists scorching, and is broad enough to make dipping easy. A less traditional option is a specialized metal pot with a ceramic insert. While water simmers in the metal pot, the cheese mixture cooks gently in the insert. Stainless-steel and enameled cast-iron pots are also good choices because they are durable, nonreactive, and hold heat well. Electric fondue pots have built-in, adjustable thermostats that allow you to make fondues right at the table.

Most fondue pots come with a stand for steadying the vessel securely above the heat source. Some stands are designed for use with a specific fuel type, so check the manufacturer's directions for guidelines. Common fuels include gels such as Sterno, denatured alcohol, butane, or even tea lights. If you are using an electric pot, set

good melting cheeses...

- Swiss-style cheeses such as Gruyère & Emmentaler
- Blue cheeses such as Roquefort & Maytag blue
- Soft-ripened cheeses such as Teleme, Brie & Camembert
- Semi-soft cheeses such as Jack, Havarti & mozzarella
- Semi-hard cheeses such as Cheddar, Edam & Manchego

it up near an outlet with the cord safely out of traffic.

ingredients

The best cheese fondues start with a good melting cheese. Any cheeses that don't melt well on their own, such as smoked Gouda or some processed cheeses, won't melt well in a fondue. Tossing a little cornstarch with the cheese prevents clumping and helps thicken the fondue to a creamy consistency. A flavorful acidic ingredient, such as dry white wine, gives the fondue depth, helps keep it creamy and smooth, and prevents it from scorching. Beer, hard cider, or fresh citrus juice can be used in place of the wine. These ingredients are the basics. Beyond them is a pantryful of herbs, spices, aromatics, such as garlic, onion, and chile, and liqueurs—including the traditional cherry-flavored kirsch—that can be used to flavor cheese fondues.

Crusty dippers, from bread cubes, pita crisps, and tortilla chips to cubes of fried polenta, are ideal for swirling in cheese fondue. Although raw vegetables are tasty in salads, most of them should be briefly cooked (blanched) in salted water until tender-crisp (see page 100) for dipping into fondue. Other flavorful dippers include pieces of warmed cooked potato or sausage.

cooking & serving

Cheese fondue is surprisingly easy to make. It can be prepared in a saucepan on the stove top and then transferred to a fondue pot for serving, or you can make it in an electric fondue pot at the table. Before you cut up or shred the cheese, always remove and discard any hard rinds or any soft

fondue rituals...

Fondue customs vary from household to household. One of the more popular traditions holds that if a diner drops a cube of bread into the fondue, he or she must kiss the person seated to his or her left.

exterior molds, such as those on Brie or Camembert, or your fondue will not be smooth. Then cut or shred the cheese finely, especially a hard cheese, so it will melt evenly.

When it is time to eat, invite diners to spear their dipper of choice onto the end of a fondue fork and plunge it into the communal pot of molten cheese. Tradition calls for stirring the cheese in a figure-eight motion across the bottom of the pot to both coat the dipper thoroughly and stir the cheese mixture. The cheese-coated morsel is then transferred to a plate, slipped free of the fondue fork, and eaten with a table fork. If the fondue becomes too thick or stringy during serving, thin it slightly by stirring in a tablespoon or two of the liquid used in the recipe.

classic swiss fondue

Emmentaler cheese, ½ lb, cut into
½-inch cubes

Gruyère cheese, ½ lb, cut into
½-inch cubes

cornstarch, 1½ tbsp

garlic, 1 clove, halved lengthwise

**dry white wine such as Alsatian
Riesling or Sauvignon Blanc,** 1¾ cups

kirsch or brandy, 2 tbsp (optional)

fresh lemon juice, 1 tbsp

freshly grated nutmeg, pinch

Kosher salt

**Accompaniments of your choice
(bottom right)**

In a bowl, toss the Emmentaler and Gruyère cheeses
with the cornstarch and set aside.

Rub the inside of a fondue pot (see page 10) with the
cut sides of the garlic halves; discard the garlic. Pour
the wine, kirsch (if using), and lemon juice into the
pot and bring to a simmer over medium-low heat.
Gradually add the cheeses, a handful at a time, and
stir gently until the mixture is creamy and the cheeses
are completely melted. Stir in the nutmeg. Taste and
adjust the seasonings, adding a little salt if needed.

When ready to serve, place the pot containing the
hot fondue in its stand in the center of the table. Light
the fuel burner according to the manufacturer's
instructions and set to low heat. Serve right away with
fondue forks and the accompaniments for dipping.

SERVES 4-6

goes great with...

- crusty bread cubes
- warmed cooked potato pieces
- warmed cooked sausage slices such
  as kielbasa, bratwurst, or linguiça
- blanched thick asparagus spears

queso fundido

Monterey jack cheese, 6 oz, cut into ½-inch cubes

sharp Cheddar cheese, 6 oz, cut into ½-inch cubes

cornstarch, 1 tbsp

ground cumin, ½ tsp

ground coriander, ½ tsp

canola oil, 1 tbsp

yellow onion, ½ cup finely chopped

garlic, 3 cloves, finely chopped

large jalapeño chile, 1, stemmed, seeded, and finely chopped

Spanish chorizo, about 3 oz, casing removed, finely chopped

green chiles, 1 can (4 oz), chopped and drained

large tomato, 1, peeled, seeded, and chopped, or ½ cup drained, canned, diced tomatoes

milk, ⅓ cup

Accompaniments of your choice (right)

In a bowl, toss the jack and Cheddar cheeses with the cornstarch, cumin, and coriander and set aside.

In a large frying pan over medium heat, warm the oil. Add the onion, garlic, jalapeño, and chorizo and sauté until the vegetables are softened, 3–4 minutes. Add the canned chiles, tomato, and milk and cook until heated through, 2–3 minutes. Gradually add the cheese mixture, a handful at a time, and stir gently until the mixture is creamy and the cheeses are completely melted.

When ready to serve, transfer the mixture to a fondue pot (see page 10) and place the pot in its stand in the center of the table. Light the fuel burner according to the manufacturer's instructions and set to low heat. Serve right away with fondue forks and the accompaniments for dipping.

SERVES 4-6

goes great with...

- Tortilla Chips, page 88, or purchased
- red or green bell pepper strips
- jicama sticks
- grilled chicken breast pieces

fontina fondue with truffle oil

fontina cheese, 1 lb, rind and hard ends removed, cut into ½-inch pieces

cornstarch, 1 tbsp

garlic, 1 clove, halved lengthwise

dry white wine such as Pinot Grigio or Verdicchio, 1 cup

fresh lemon juice, 2 tbsp

grappa or kirsch, 2 tbsp

finely ground white pepper, ¼ tsp

white truffle oil, 3 tsp

Accompaniments of your choice (bottom right)

In a bowl, toss the fontina cheese with the cornstarch and set aside.

Rub the inside of a fondue pot (see page 10) with the cut sides of the garlic halves; discard the garlic. Pour the wine, lemon juice, and grappa into the pot and bring to a low simmer over medium-low heat. Gradually add the cheese, a handful at a time, and stir gently until the mixture is creamy and the cheese is completely melted. Stir in the white pepper and truffle oil.

When ready to serve, place the pot containing the hot fondue in its stand in the center of the table. Light the fuel burner according to the manufacturer's instructions and set to low heat. Serve right away with fondue forks and the accompaniments for dipping.

SERVES 4

goes great with...

- blanched broccoli florets
- warmed cooked potato pieces
- Polenta Cubes, page 88
- crusty baguette or focaccia cubes
- cooked tortellini
- red bell pepper squares

edam fondue with bacon & smothered onions

Edam cheese, ½ lb, rind removed, cut into ½-inch cubes

Monterey jack cheese, ½ lb, cut into ½-inch cubes

cornstarch, 2 tbsp

thick-cut bacon, 3 oz (about 2 slices), cut into ¼-inch pieces

yellow onion, ½ cup finely diced

garlic, 1 clove, finely chopped

dry white wine such as Muscadet or Alsatian Riesling, 1½ cups

sherry vinegar, 2 tbsp

red hot-pepper sauce such as Tabasco, dash

Accompaniments of your choice (below)

goes great with...

- crusty bread cubes
- warmed cooked potato pieces
- warmed cooked sausage slices such as linguiça
- cooked pork or beef tenderloin cubes
- crisp apple chunks

In a bowl, toss the Edam and jack cheeses with the cornstarch and set aside.

In a large frying pan over medium heat, sauté the bacon until beginning to brown, about 5 minutes. Add the onion and cook until softened but not brown, about 3 minutes. Add the garlic and cook just until fragrant, about 30 seconds. Carefully spoon off most of the rendered fat and discard. Add the wine, vinegar, and pepper sauce and bring to a low simmer. Gradually add the cheeses, a handful at a time, and stir gently until the mixture is creamy and the cheeses are completely melted.

When ready to serve, transfer the mixture to a fondue pot (see page 10) and place the pot in its stand in the center of the table. Light the fuel burner according to the manufacturer's instructions and set to low heat. Serve right away with fondue forks and the accompaniments for dipping.

SERVES 4

pepper jack fondue with roasted garlic

garlic, 1 large head, unpeeled and left whole, plus 1 clove garlic, halved lengthwise

olive oil

pepper jack cheese, ¾ lb, coarsely shredded

sharp Cheddar cheese, 2 oz, cut into ½-inch cubes

cornstarch, 1 tbsp

ground cumin, 1 tsp

dry mustard powder, ½ tsp

dry white wine such as Sauvignon Blanc, 1⅓ cups

tequila, 2 tbsp

fresh lime or lemon juice, 1 tbsp

Accompaniments of your choice (below)

goes great with...

- Tortilla Chips, page 88, or purchased
- jicama sticks
- bell pepper squares

Preheat the oven to 375°F. Cut a ½-inch slice off the top of the garlic head to expose the cloves and brush with oil. Wrap the garlic head in aluminum foil and roast until very tender when pierced with a small knife, 50–60 minutes. Unwrap and let cool. When cool to the touch, squeeze each clove from its skin into a small bowl. Using a fork, mash the cloves until almost smooth; you should have about 2 tablespoons.

In a bowl, toss the jack and Cheddar cheeses with the cornstarch, cumin, and mustard and set aside.

Rub the inside of a fondue pot (see page 10) with the cut sides of the remaining garlic clove; discard the garlic. Pour the wine, tequila, and lime juice into the pot and bring to a low simmer over medium-low heat. Stir in the roasted garlic. Gradually add the cheeses, a handful at a time, and stir gently until the mixture is creamy and the cheeses are completely melted.

When ready to serve, place the pot containing the hot fondue in its stand in the center of the table. Light the fuel burner according to the manufacturer's instructions and set the heat to low. Serve right away with fondue forks and the accompaniments for dipping.

SERVES 4

parmesan & artichoke dip fondue

frozen artichoke hearts, 1 package (8 oz)

Parmesan cheese, 6 oz, freshly grated

Emmentaler cheese, ¼ lb, cut into ½-inch cubes

whipped cream cheese, ¼ lb

cornstarch, 1 tbsp

butter, 1 tbsp

garlic, 2 large cloves, finely chopped

green onions, 5–6, white and pale green parts only, finely chopped

dry white wine such as Orvieto or Sauvignon Blanc, 1–1¼ cups

fresh lemon juice, ¼ cup

red hot-pepper sauce such as Tabasco, ¼ tsp

Accompaniments of your choice (below)

goes great with...

- Baked Pita Strips, page 88, or purchased
- celery sticks
- blanched sugar snap peas
- endive leaves

In a saucepan of boiling salted water, simmer the artichokes until tender, about 6 minutes; drain and let cool slightly. When cool to the touch, finely chop the artichokes and set aside.

In a bowl, mix together the Parmesan, Emmentaler, cream cheese, and cornstarch and set aside.

In a large frying pan over low heat, melt the butter. Add the garlic and green onions and sauté until softened, 2–3 minutes. Add the chopped artichoke hearts, 1 cup of the wine, the lemon juice, and pepper sauce and bring to a low simmer. Gradually add the cheese mixture, a handful at a time, and stir gently until the mixture is creamy and the cheeses are completely melted. If the mixture is too thick, stir in the remaining wine as needed to create a good dipping consistency.

When ready to serve, transfer the mixture to a fondue pot (see page 10) and place the pot in its stand in the center of the table. Light the fuel burner according to the manufacturer's instructions and set to low heat. Serve right away with fondue forks and the accompaniments for dipping.

SERVES 4-6

blue cheese fondue with port-glazed shallots

blue cheese, ½ lb, crumbled, plus more for garnish

Havarti cheese, ½ lb, cut into ½-inch cubes

cornstarch, 2 tbsp

unsalted butter, 1 tbsp

shallot, 1, minced (about 3 tbsp)

tawny or ruby Port, ½ cup

balsamic or sherry vinegar, 2 tbsp

milk, ½ cup, plus 1–2 tbsp as needed

Accompaniments of your choice (below)

goes great with...

- crusty bread cubes
- cooked lamb or beef tenderloin pieces
- warmed cooked potato pieces, in a variety of colors, if desired
- Grilled Apples, page 89
- red and green Belgian endive leaves
- blanched broccoli or cauliflower florets

In a bowl, toss the blue and Havarti cheeses with the cornstarch and set aside.

In a large frying pan over medium heat, melt the butter. Add the shallot and sauté until it begins to caramelize, 2–3 minutes. Raise the heat to medium-high, add the Port and vinegar, and cook, stirring and scraping up the browned bits on the bottom of the pan, until slightly reduced, 2–3 minutes. Reduce the heat to medium-low, add the ½ cup milk and cook until warmed through, 2 minutes. Gradually add the cheeses, a handful at a time, and stir gently until the mixture is creamy and the cheeses are completely melted. If the mixture is too thick, stir in the 1–2 tablepoons milk as needed to create a good dipping consistency.

When ready to serve, transfer the mixture to a fondue pot (see page 10), sprinkle the fondue with crumbled blue cheese, and place the pot in its stand in the center of the table. Light the fuel burner according to the manufacturer's instructions and set to low heat. Serve right away with fondue forks and the accompaniments for dipping.

SERVES 4

normandy-style fondue

Camembert cheese, 1 lb

Monterey jack or Havarti cheese, ¼ lb, coarsely shredded

cornstarch, 1½ tbsp

unsalted butter, 2 tbsp

shallot, ¼ cup minced

dry, hard apple cider or white wine, 1–1¼ cups

fresh lemon juice, 2 tbsp

Calvados or apple brandy, 2 tbsp

freshly ground white pepper, pinch

Accompaniments of your choice (below)

goes great with...

- crusty bread cubes
- warmed cooked potato pieces
- warmed cooked sausage slices such as garlic sausage or bratwurst
- ham chunks

Place the Camembert in the freezer for 30 minutes to firm the cheese. Using a sharp knife, carefully cut away and discard the rind, then coarsely chop the cheese. Toss the Camembert and jack cheeses with the cornstarch and set aside.

In a large frying pan over medium-low heat, melt the butter. Add the shallot and sauté until soft and translucent, about 3 minutes. Add 1 cup of the cider, the lemon juice, Calvados, and pepper and bring to a low simmer. Gradually add the cheeses, a handful at a time, and stir gently until the mixture is creamy and the cheeses are completely melted. If the mixture is too thick, stir in the remaining ¼ cup cider as needed to create a good dipping consistency.

When ready to serve, transfer the mixture to a fondue pot (see page 10) and place the pot in its stand in the center of the table. Light the fuel burner according to the manufacturer's instructions and set to low heat. Serve right away with fondue forks and the accompaniments for dipping.

SERVES 4

cream cheese & crabmeat fondue

dry white wine such as Sauvignon Blanc or Alsatian Riesling, 1¼ cups

celery, ½ cup minced

red bell pepper, ½ cup minced

green onions, 4, white parts only, finely chopped

Old Bay seasoning, 2 tbsp

fresh lemon juice, 1 tbsp

jalapeño chile, seeded, if desired, 1–2 tsp finely minced

Freshly ground pepper

whipped cream cheese, 1 lb

milk, ½–⅔ cup

cooked fresh crabmeat, ½ lb, picked over and pulled into small pieces

Accompaniments of your choice (bottom right)

In a large frying pan over medium-low heat, combine the wine, celery, bell pepper, green onions, Old Bay seasoning, lemon juice, jalapeño, and pepper to taste and bring to a low simmer. Gradually add the cream cheese, a spoonful at a time, and stir gently until the mixture is creamy and the cheese is completely melted. Add ½ cup of the milk and the crabmeat and cook until heated through, 3–4 minutes. If the mixture is too thick, stir in the remaining milk as needed to create a good dipping consistency and continue cooking until well blended, 1–2 minutes longer.

When ready to serve, transfer the mixture to a fondue pot (see page 10) and place the pot in its stand in the center of the table. Light the fuel burner according to the manufacturer's instructions and set to low heat. Serve right away with fondue forks and the accompaniments for dipping.

SERVES 4

goes great with...

- carrot sticks, radishes, bell pepper squares, cucumber chunks, or blanched broccoli or cauliflower florets
- Baked Pita Strips, page 88, or purchased
- Tortilla Chips, page 88, or purchased
- crusty bread cubes

manchego fondue with piquillo peppers & toasted garlic

Manchego cheese, ½ lb, coarsely shredded

Monterey jack cheese, ½ lb, cut into ½-inch cubes

cornstarch, 2 tbsp

sweet paprika, preferably Spanish, 2 tsp

extra-virgin olive oil, 1 tbsp

garlic, 4 cloves, thinly sliced

dry white wine such as white Rioja or Albariño, 1½ cups

red hot-pepper sauce such as Tabasco, dash

jarred piquillo peppers, ½ cup finely chopped

Accompaniments of your choice (bottom right)

In a bowl, toss the Manchego and jack cheeses with the cornstarch and paprika and set aside.

In a large frying pan over medium-low heat, warm the oil. Add the garlic and sauté until just beginning to color, 2–3 minutes. Add the wine and pepper sauce and bring to a low simmer. Gradually add the cheese mixture, a handful at a time, and stir gently until the mixture is creamy and the cheeses are completely melted. Stir in the peppers.

When ready to serve, transfer the mixture to a fondue pot (see page 10) and place the pot in its stand in the center of the table. Light the fuel burner according to the manufacturer's instructions and set to low heat. Serve right away with fondue forks and the accompaniments for dipping.

SERVES 4

goes great with...

- warmed Spanish chorizo slices
- blanched cauliflower or broccoli florets
- blanched thick asparagus spears
- roasted chicken pieces
- crusty bread cubes

smoked salmon fondue with cream cheese & dill

aquavit or vodka, 3 tbsp

fresh lemon juice, 1 tbsp

whipped cream cheese, ¾ lb

smoked salmon, 6 oz, cut into ½-inch pieces

fresh dill, ¼ cup chopped

red hot-pepper sauce such as Tabasco, 3 or 4 drops

milk, 1–2 tbsp

Accompaniments of your choice (below)

goes great with...

- thin rye bread slices or bagel chunks, lightly toasted, if desired
- English cucumber slices
- yellow or red bell pepper squares
- blanched sugar snap peas

In a fondue pot or saucepan over medium-low heat, combine the aquavit, lemon juice, and cream cheese and bring to a low simmer. Cook, stirring, until the mixture is creamy and the cheese is melted.

Stir in the smoked salmon, dill, and pepper sauce and cook until heated through, about 1 minute. Stir in the milk as needed to create a smooth, creamy dipping consistency.

When ready to serve, place the pot containing the hot fondue in its stand in the center of the table. Or, if desired, transfer the fondue to 2 or more small, attractive, flameproof pots and set on a sturdy stand over a fuel burner or on a trivet set over tea lights. Light the fuel burner according to the manufacturer's instructions and set to low heat. Serve at once with fondue forks and the accompaniments for dipping.

SERVES 4-6

french onion soup fondue

yellow onions, 1½ lb

extra-virgin olive oil, 2 tbsp

kosher salt, ½ tsp

fresh thyme, leaves from 2 sprigs

sugar, 1 tsp

Gruyère cheese, ¾ lb, cut into ½-inch cubes

cornstarch, 2 tsp

Beef Stock (page 97) or reduced-sodium beef broth, ¾ cup

dry white wine such as Muscadet or Sauvignon Blanc, ½ cup

Cognac, 2 tbsp

fresh lemon juice, 1 tbsp

Accompaniments of your choice (below)

goes great with...

- crusty bread cubes
- cooked beef or pork tenderloin pieces
- Grilled Apples, page 89, or raw apple or pear wedges

Cut the onions into quarters and thinly slice each quarter crosswise; you should have 6–7 cups. In a large frying pan over medium heat, warm the oil. Add the onions, salt, and thyme. Cover and cook, stirring the mixture 2 or 3 times, until the onions are very soft, about 15 minutes. Uncover, raise the heat to medium-high, and sprinkle with the sugar. Continue to cook, stirring frequently to prevent burning, until the onions are golden brown and caramelized, 10–15 minutes longer. Set aside.

In a bowl, toss the Gruyère cheese with the cornstarch and set aside.

In a fondue pot (see page 10) over medium-low heat, combine the Beef Stock, wine, Cognac, and lemon juice and bring to a low simmer. Gradually add the cheese, a handful at a time, and stir gently until the mixture is creamy and the cheese is completely melted. Add the caramelized onions and stir to combine. If the mixture is too thick, stir in 1–2 tablespoons water as needed to create a good dipping consistency. Taste and adjust the seasonings with more salt, if desired.

When ready to serve, place the pot containing the hot fondue in its stand in the center of the table. Light the fuel burner according to the manufacturer's instructions and set to low heat. Serve right away with fondue forks and the accompaniments for dipping.

SERVES 4

southwestern layered fondue

thick-cut bacon, 3 oz (about 2 slices)

sharp Cheddar cheese, 2 oz, coarsely shredded

cornstarch, 1 tsp

dry mustard, ¼ tsp

avocado, 1, halved and pitted

fresh lime juice, 1 tbsp

Kosher salt and freshly ground pepper

refried beans, 1 cup

sour cream, ½ cup

corn kernels, 1 cup cooked

prepared chunky tomato salsa, ⅔ cup

sliced black olives, 1 can (2½ oz), drained

half-and-half, ½ cup

canned chipotle chile in adobo sauce, ½ tsp chopped, or to taste

fresh cilantro leaves, 2 tbsp chopped

Accompaniments of your choice (below)

goes great with...

- Tortilla Chips, page 88, or purchased
- bell pepper squares
- grilled chicken breast pieces

In a small frying pan over medium heat, sauté the bacon until crisp, about 5 minutes. Transfer to a paper towel–lined plate. When cool, crumble and set aside.

In a bowl, toss the cheese with the cornstarch and mustard and set aside.

Scoop the avocado flesh into a bowl and add the lime juice and salt and pepper to taste. Using a fork, mash the mixture together to form a coarse paste.

Preheat the oven to 350°F. In a small bowl, combine the refried beans, sour cream, and crumbled bacon and mix well. Spread the mixture in the bottom of a shallow 9-inch, ovenproof serving dish. Top with the corn, spreading it in an even layer. Repeat with the salsa, avocado mixture, and olives, spreading each into an even layer. Place the baking dish in the oven and bake for 10–15 minutes to warm through.

Meanwhile, in a small saucepan over medium-low heat, bring the half-and-half to a simmer. Add the cheese mixture and chipotle chile and stir gently until the mixture is creamy and the cheese is completely melted.

Remove the baking dish from the oven, spoon the cheese mixture over the top, and garnish with the cilantro. Serve at once with fondue forks and the accompaniments for dipping.

SERVES 4

brie fondue with mushrooms & herbs

Brie cheese, 1 lb

Havarti cheese, ¼ lb, cut into ½-inch cubes

cornstarch, 1 tbsp

garlic, 1 clove, halved lengthwise

dry white wine such as Albariño or Sauvignon Blanc, ¾–1 cup

fresh lemon juice, 1 tbsp

brandy or dry sherry, 2 tbsp

Mushroom-Herb Paste (page 92), 1½ cups

fresh flat-leaf parsley, 3 tbsp finely chopped

chives, 1 tbsp minced

Accompaniments of your choice (below)

goes great with...

- crusty bread cubes
- Caramelized Shallot Halves, page 89
- warmed cooked potato pieces
- blanched thick asparagus spears

Place the Brie in the freezer for 30 minutes to firm the cheese. Using a sharp knife, carefully cut away and discard the rind, then cut the cheese into 1-inch pieces. In a bowl, toss the Brie and Havarti cheeses with the cornstarch and set aside.

Rub the inside of a fondue pot (see page 10) with the cut sides of the garlic halves; discard the garlic. Pour ¾ cup of the wine, the lemon juice, and brandy into the pot and bring to a low simmer over medium-low heat. Gradually add the cheeses, a handful at a time, and stir gently until the mixture is creamy and the cheeses are completely melted. Stir in the Mushroom-Herb Paste. If the mixture is too thick, stir in the remaining wine as needed to create a good dipping consistency. Stir in the parsley and chives.

When ready to serve, place the pot containing the hot fondue in its stand in the center of the table. Light the fuel burner according to the manufacturer's instructions and set to low heat. Serve right away with fondue forks and the accompaniments for dipping.

SERVES 4

cheddar & ale fondue

sharp Cheddar cheese, ¾ lb, cut into ½-inch cubes

cornstarch, 1 tbsp

dry mustard powder, ½ tsp

sweet paprika, ½ tsp

unsalted butter, 2 tbsp

garlic, 1 clove, finely chopped

pale ale or pilsner, ¾ cup

Worcestershire sauce, 1 tsp

Accompaniments of your choice (below)

goes great with...

- apple wedges
- crusty bread cubes, lightly toasted, if desired
- warmed cooked potato pieces
- warmed cooked sausage slices such as Polish sausage, Italian sausage, or linguiça
- cocktail franks

In a bowl, toss the cheese with the cornstarch, mustard, and paprika and set aside.

In a frying pan over medium-low heat, melt the butter. Add the garlic and sauté until softened, 1–2 minutes. Pour in the ale and Worcestershire sauce and bring to a low simmer. Gradually add the cheese, a handful at a time, and stir gently until the mixture is creamy and the cheese is completely melted.

When ready to serve, transfer the mixture to a fondue pot (see page 10) and place the pot in its stand in the center of the table. Light the fuel burner according to the manufacturer's instructions and set to low heat. Serve right away with fondue forks and the accompaniments for dipping.

SERVES 4

provolone fondue with sun-dried tomato pesto

pine nuts, ¼ cup chopped

oil-packed sun-dried tomatoes,
7–8, coarsely chopped

garlic, 3 large cloves, coarsely chopped

fresh flat-leaf parsley leaves, ⅓ cup
lightly packed

Parmesan cheese, 1 tbsp freshly grated

extra-virgin olive oil, 1–2 tsp

provolone cheese, ¾ lb, shredded

whole-milk mozzarella cheese,
¼ lb, shredded

cornstarch, 1 tbsp

**dry white wine such as Pinot Grigio
or Sauvignon Blanc,** 1 cup

fresh lemon juice, 2 tbsp

red hot-pepper sauce such as Tabasco,
½ tsp or to taste

**Accompaniments of your choice
(below)**

goes great with...

- Polenta Cubes, page 88,
  pan-fried until golden,
  if desired
- cherry tomatoes
- fennel slices

To make the sun-dried tomato pesto, in a small dry frying pan over medium heat, toast the pine nuts, shaking the pan occasionally, until fragrant and lightly browned, about 3 minutes. Transfer the nuts to a plate and let cool to room temperature.

In a food processor, combine the toasted pine nuts, sun-dried tomatoes, garlic, and parsley. Process for about 30 seconds, scraping down the sides of the bowl once or twice. Add the Parmesan cheese and oil and process until combined, about 5 seconds longer.

In a bowl, toss the provolone and mozzarella cheeses with the cornstarch and set aside.

In a frying pan over medium-low heat, combine the wine, lemon juice, and pepper sauce and bring to a low simmer. Gradually add the cheeses, a handful at a time, and stir gently until the mixture is creamy and the cheeses are completely melted. Stir in the sun-dried tomato pesto.

When ready to serve, transfer the mixture to a fondue pot (see page 10) and place the pot in its stand in the center of the table. Light the fuel burner according to the manufacturer's instructions and set to low heat. Serve right away with fondue forks and the accompaniments for dipping.

SERVES 4

about oil fondues 40

shrimp & scallop fondue with chipotle tartar sauce 43

chicken fondue with spicy peanut sauce 44

marinated ahi fondue with wasabi dipping sauce 45

pork fondue with mango relish 46

bagna cauda 49

sausage & potato fondue with honey-mustard sauce 50

swordfish fondue with lemon-caper rémoulade 51

beef fondue with creamy horseradish sauce 53

oil fondues

about oil fondues

Fondue bourguignonne, small cubes of tender beef cooked in hot oil, originated in France during the 1500s as a quick lunch for vineyard workers. Oil fondues have since evolved to include other meats, as well as seafood and poultry, and a varied menu of dipping sauces that draws on ingredients from around the world.

equipment

The ideal pot for oil fondues is an electric fondue pot with an adjustable thermostat that will keep the oil at the optimal temperature throughout the meal. The oil must be at a constant 350° to 375°F. If it is cooler, the food will absorb too much oil before it cooks through. To ensure the oil temperature matches the thermostat setting, clip a deep-frying thermometer onto the side of pot and check it often.

The best electric pots have a metal ring that rests on top and prevents the oil from spattering diners. These guards usually have grooves for resting fondue forks while the foods are cooking. Also, use fondue forks with wooden handles for oil fondues. Metal handles can get too hot for guests to grasp.

ingredients

Peanut and canola oils are good choices for oil fondues for two reasons: they can be heated to high temperatures before they begin to break down and smoke, and the

oil fondue safety...

Never transport heated oil from your stove top to the fondue pot, or try to move an electric pot filled with hot oil. Instead, place the electric pot in the center of a stable table, and then pour the oil into the pot and heat it.

neutral flavor of canola oil and the mildly nutty flavor of peanut oil won't overpower the taste of the food being dipped.

Most meats, poultry, and shellfish are suitable for oil fondues. If cooking fin fish, choose a firm, meaty type, such as tuna or swordfish.

cooking & serving

When you are ready to begin, place the fondue pot on a heavy metal tray or washable tablecloth in the center of the table, positioned so that all of the guests can reach it easily. Pour the oil into the pot, filling it no more than half full. You'll need 2 to 3 cups, depending on the size of the pot. Next, plug in the electrical cord and turn on the temperature control to the desired temperature, typically 375°F.

Meanwhile, set the table, providing the following for each guest: a small plate, a fondue fork, a table fork, a napkin, a small dish for the dipping sauce, and a paper towel–lined small plate for blotting the food as it comes out of the oil. Set out the ingredients to be cooked, making sure you have patted them dry before arranging them on a platter, as excess moisture can cause the oil to spatter.

When the oil reaches the desired temperature, gather your guests at the table and begin the meal. Invite them to skewer a piece of food onto a fondue fork and immerse it in the hot oil until cooked through, usually 20 to 50 seconds for seafood, 30 to 60 seconds for meats, and 1 to 2 minutes for poultry.

It is important that the oil temperature doesn't drop dramatically during the cooking process, so suggest that only 2 to 3 pieces of food be cooked at a time. Next,

delicious dipping...

Each recipe is paired with a specific dipping sauce, but don't feel limited to these suggestions. Look through pages 92 through 96 for an array of dipping sauces that you can mix and match according to your own taste.

instruct diners to blot their cooked morsels briefly on their towel-lined plates to remove excess oil, and then to remove them from the fondue forks to avoid burning their mouths. Guests use their table forks to swirl the food in the dipping sauce and eat it.

Allow the oil to return to the optimal temperature between batches, making sure it doesn't get too hot or it can burst into flame. Adjust the thermostat or other heat source as needed throughout cooking.

Oil deteriorates at high temperatures, so once your guests have finished eating, let the oil cool completely, then pour it into an empty milk carton, plastic bottle, or jar with a lid, seal it tightly, and throw it away in your trash. Or, check to see if your city accepts used cooking oil for recycling.

shrimp & scallop fondue with chipotle tartar sauce

canola or peanut oil, 2–3 cups

large shrimp, ¾ lb, peeled and deveined

medium-sized sea scallops, ¾ lb

rice flour or all-purpose flour, ¼ cup

kosher salt, 1 tsp

sweet paprika, 1 tsp

cayenne pepper, ¼ tsp

Chipotle Tartar Sauce (page 95)

serving tip...

Make the tartar sauce at least an hour before you plan to serve it to allow the flavors to develop. Serve the fondue alongside steamed new potatoes and asparagus, both of which are delicious dipped into the creamy sauce.

Assemble an electric fondue pot in the center of the table and pour enough of the oil into the pot to reach no more than halfway up the sides. Set the temperature control to medium-high and warm the oil until it reads 375°F on a deep-frying thermometer.

Pat the shrimp and scallops dry with paper towels. On a shallow plate, stir together the flour, salt, paprika, and cayenne. Just before serving, lightly coat the shellfish in the seasoned flour, shaking off any excess, and transfer to a platter. Spoon the Chipotle Tartar Sauce into individual ramekins or a serving bowl.

Instruct diners to do the following: Cook a shrimp or scallop in the hot oil until lightly browned and opaque throughout, 30–40 seconds, depending on the size of the shellfish (see page 41). Only 2 or 3 shrimp or scallops should be cooked at one time to maintain the proper oil temperature. Blot the shellfish briefly on a paper towel–lined plate and enjoy right away with the tartar sauce.

SERVES 4

chicken fondue with spicy peanut sauce

lime zest, freshly grated from 1 lime

fresh lime juice, 3 tbsp

soy sauce, 3 tbsp

brown sugar, 1½ tbsp firmly packed

garlic, 1 clove, minced

skinless, boneless chicken breasts,
1 lb, cut into ¼-inch slices or
¾-inch chunks

canola or peanut oil, 2–3 cups

Spicy Peanut Sauce (page 93),
warmed

Chopped fresh cilantro for garnish

serving tip...

This fondue is inspired by
Southeast Asian chicken satay,
with fondue forks instead of
wood skewers holding the meat
as it cooks. The chicken is also
delicious paired with Mango
Relish (page 92) or Pineapple-
Chile Salsa (page 93).

In a shallow glass or ceramic dish, combine the lime zest and juice, soy sauce, brown sugar, and garlic. Add the chicken chunks and toss to coat evenly. Let stand at room temperature for 10–15 minutes.

Assemble an electric fondue pot in the center of the table and pour enough of the oil into the pot to reach no more than halfway up the sides. Set the temperature control to medium-high and warm the oil until it reads 375°F on a deep-frying thermometer.

Remove the chicken chunks from the marinade, pat dry with paper towels, and arrange on a platter. (Alternatively, thread each piece onto an 8-inch wooden or metal skewer and arrange on the platter.) Spoon the Spicy Peanut Sauce into 4 individual ramekins or a serving bowl and garnish with the chopped cilantro.

Instruct diners to do the following: Cook a piece of chicken in the hot oil until it is no longer pink when cut into with a knife, 1–2 minutes (see page 41). Only 2 or 3 pieces of chicken should be cooked at one time to maintain the proper oil temperature. Blot the chicken briefly on a paper towel–lined plate and enjoy right away with the peanut sauce.

SERVES 4

marinated ahi fondue with wasabi dipping sauce

soy sauce, 2 tbsp

fresh ginger, ½ tsp grated

Asian sesame oil, ½ tsp

ahi tuna, 1¼ lb, cut into 1½-inch chunks

canola or peanut oil, 2–3 cups

Wasabi Dipping Sauce (page 95)

serving tip...

This is the perfect fondue for sashimi lovers. For rare tuna, you only need to cook it in the oil for about 10–15 seconds, just long enough to sear the outside. Pass extra wasabi paste at the table for those who want their dipping sauce extra spicy.

In a shallow glass or ceramic dish, combine the soy sauce, ginger, and sesame oil. Add the tuna chunks and turn to coat evenly. Let stand at room temperature while you warm the canola oil.

Assemble an electric fondue pot in the center of the table and pour enough of the canola oil into the pot to reach no more than halfway up the sides. Set the temperature control to medium-high and warm the oil until it reads 375°F on a deep-frying thermometer.

Remove the tuna pieces from the marinade, pat dry with paper towels, and arrange on a platter. Spoon the Wasabi Dipping Sauce into 4 individual ramekins or a serving bowl.

Instruct diners to do the following: Cook a piece of tuna in the hot oil until seared on the outside but still pink in the center, 20–30 seconds, or cooked to their liking (see page 41). Only 2 or 3 pieces of fish should be cooked at one time to maintain the proper oil temperature. Blot the tuna briefly on a paper towel–lined plate and enjoy right away with the dipping sauce.

SERVES 4

pork fondue with mango relish

soy sauce, 2 tbsp

Chinese rice wine, 1 tbsp

finely ground white pepper, ⅛ tsp

ground allspice, 1 tsp

pork tenderloin, 1, about 1 lb,
trimmed and cut into ⅛-inch slices or
1-inch cubes

canola or peanut oil, 2–3 cups

Mango Relish (page 92)

serving tip...

You can make the relish several
days in advance and refrigerate
it, but be sure to bring it to room
temperature before serving. It is
also delicious when warmed,
sprinkled with fresh cilantro
leaves, and served with a lime
wedge for squeezing over the top.

In a shallow glass or ceramic dish, combine the soy
sauce, rice wine, pepper, and allspice. Add the pork
and turn to coat evenly. Let stand at room temperature
for 20–30 minutes.

Assemble an electric fondue pot in the center of the
table and pour enough of the oil into the pot to reach
no more than halfway up the sides. Set the temperature
control to medium-high and warm the oil until it reads
375°F on a deep-frying thermometer.

Remove the pork pieces from the marinade, pat them
dry with paper towels, and arrange them on a platter.
(Alternatively, thread the pork pieces onto 8-inch
wooden or metal skewers and arrange on the platter.)
Spoon the Mango Relish into 4 individual ramekins
or a serving bowl.

Instruct diners to do the following: Cook a piece of pork
in the hot oil until lightly browned, 40–60 seconds,
or until cooked to their liking (see page 41). Only 2 or
3 pieces of pork should be cooked at one time to
maintain the proper oil temperature. Blot the pork
briefly on a paper towel–lined plate and enjoy right
away with the relish.

SERVES 4

bagna cauda

unsalted butter, ½ cup

extra-virgin olive oil, ½ cup

oil-packed whole anchovies, 5 or 6, rinsed, dried, and chopped

garlic, 4 or 5 cloves, finely chopped or pressed

red pepper flakes, 1–2 pinches

capers, 2 tbsp, drained and minced

kosher salt, ½ tsp

cooked artichoke leaves and hearts, from 2 steamed artichokes, hearts cut into bite-sized pieces

radishes, 8–10, halved

small carrots, 6–8, in a variety of colors, if desired, cut into sticks

baby zucchini or yellow squashes, 4–6, halved

crusty French bread, 1 loaf, cut into 2-inch pieces

In a small saucepan over medium-low heat, melt the butter with the oil. Reduce the heat to low, add the anchovies, garlic, and red pepper flakes, and cook, stirring frequently, until the anchovies break up, about 10 minutes. Stir in the capers and salt.

Pour the mixture into a warmed flameproof serving dish and set on the table on a stand or raised trivet over a tea light to keep warm. Arrange the artichoke leaves and hearts, radishes, carrots, and zucchini on a platter and place alongside the dip.

Instruct diners to do the following: Dip a vegetable into the oil mixture and warm until heated through, 20–30 seconds. Hold a crusty piece of bread under each dipped vegetable to catch any drips while transferring the vegetable to the plate.

SERVES 6

more accompaniments...

- cooked small potatoes, quartered
- halved mushrooms
- sliced raw fennel
- broccoli or cauliflower florets
- blanched sugar snap peas
- large squares of red or yellow bell pepper

sausage & potato fondue with honey-mustard sauce

Kosher salt

creamer potatoes, 1 lb, about 2 inches in diameter

canola or peanut oil, 2–3 cups

fully cooked sausages such as bratwurst, kielbasa, or linguiça, 1¼ lb, cut into ¾- to 1-inch slices

Honey-Mustard Sauce (page 94)

serving tip...

Host your own fall fête with this fondue as the centerpiece. Serve the fondue with a selection of German beers, a platter of pickled vegetables, pretzels, and hearty bread.

In a saucepan of boiling salted water, cook the unpeeled whole potatoes until tender when pierced with a small knife, about 25 minutes. Drain well and let cool. Halve the cooled potatoes and set aside.

Assemble an electric fondue pot in the center of the table and pour enough of the oil into the pot to reach no more than halfway up the sides. Set the temperature control to medium-high and warm the oil until it reads 375°F on a deep-frying thermometer.

Arrange the cooked potato halves and sausage slices on a platter. Spoon the Honey-Mustard Sauce into 4 individual ramekins or a serving bowl.

Instruct diners to do the following: Cook a piece of potato or sausage in the hot oil until lightly browned on the outside and warmed through, 30–40 seconds, or until cooked to their liking (see page 41). Only 2 or 3 pieces of potato or sausage should be cooked at one time to maintain the proper oil temperature. Blot the pieces briefly on a paper towel–lined plate and enjoy right away with the mustard sauce.

SERVES 4

swordfish fondue with lemon-caper rémoulade

canola or peanut oil, 2–3 cups

thick swordfish steaks, 1¼ lb, cut into 1-inch cubes

Lemon-Caper Rémoulade (page 95)

serving tip...

Try to seek out swordfish caught using sustainable fishing methods; ask your fishmonger to be sure. You can also substitute thick pieces of halibut or other firm-fleshed white fish for the swordfish.

Assemble an electric fondue pot in the center of the table and pour enough of the oil into the pot to reach no more than halfway up the sides. Set the temperature control to medium-high and warm the oil until it reads 375°F on a deep-frying thermometer.

Pat the fish dry and arrange on a platter. Spoon the Lemon-Caper Rémoulade into 4 individual ramekins or a serving bowl.

Instruct diners to do the following: Cook a piece of swordfish in the hot oil until lightly browned on the outside and opaque throughout, 40–50 seconds, or until cooked to their liking (see page 41). Only 3 or 4 pieces of fish should be cooked at one time to maintain the proper oil temperature. Blot the fish briefly on a paper towel–lined plate and enjoy right away with the rémoulade.

SERVES 4

beef fondue with creamy horseradish sauce

soy sauce, 2 tbsp

dry sherry, 2 tbsp

Worcestershire sauce, 2 tsp

beef tenderloin or top-sirloin steak,
1¼ lb, trimmed and cut into slices
¼-inch thick by 2 inches long

canola or peanut oil, 2–3 cups

Creamy Horseradish Sauce (page 94)

Kosher salt and freshly ground pepper

serving tip...

This fondue plays on the classic
pairing of beef with horseradish.
Roasted sweet potato wedges
and steamed asparagus spears
are nice accompaniments to
round out the meal.

In a shallow glass or ceramic dish, combine the soy sauce, sherry, and Worcestershire sauce. Add the beef slices and turn to coat evenly. Let stand at room temperature while you warm the oil.

Assemble an electric fondue pot in the center of the table and pour enough of the oil into the pot to reach no more than halfway up the sides. Set the temperature control to medium-high and warm the oil until it reads 375°F on a deep-frying thermometer.

Remove the beef slices from the marinade, pat them dry with paper towels, and arrange them on a platter. (Alternatively, thread each slice onto an 8-inch wooden or metal skewer and arrange on the platter.) Taste the horseradish sauce and adjust the seasonings with salt and pepper. Spoon into 4 individual ramekins or a serving bowl.

Instruct diners to do the following: Cook a piece of beef in the hot oil until lightly browned, 30–40 seconds for medium-rare or until cooked to their liking (see page 41). Only 2 or 3 pieces of beef should be cooked at one time to maintain the proper oil temperature. Blot the beef briefly on a paper towel–lined plate and enjoy right away with the horseradish sauce.

SERVES 4

about broth fondues 56

sichuan hot pot 59

mongolian hot pot 60

vietnamese beef & vinegar hot pot 61

shabu-shabu 62

chicken fondue with romesco sauce 65

thai curry hot pot with seafood 66

broth fondues

about broth fondues

Broth fondues have long graced tables in Asia, where the tradition of family meals remains strong. Commonly known as hot pots, steamboats, or firepots, these communal dishes vary according to the occasion, the time of year, and the country. Here, you'll find recipes from Japan, China, Vietnam, and Thailand, along with a Spanish-style chicken fondue.

equipment

A thermostatically controlled electric hot pot, skillet, or wok works well for broth fondues. A metal hot pot with a central chimney, also known as a shabu-shabu pot, can also be used. Traditionally, this pot is fueled by charcoal, but modern versions are available that use an electric hot plate or a gas burner. You can also use a stainless-steel or enameled cast-iron fondue pot, as long as the heat source—a gel-type fuel such as Sterno, an alcohol burner, or an electric hot plate—burns hot enough to keep the broth at a simmer.

ingredients

Ingredients can be as simple as a single meat and a couple of vegetables, or as extravagant as several types of seafood, a bouquet of mixed herbs, a few vegetables, rice stick noodles, and mushrooms. If some of the ingredients in the following recipes are unfamiliar, don't be discouraged. Once you have purchased them, you'll find

yourself adding many of them to other hot pots or Asian dishes. Asian markets and well-stocked supermarkets are the best sources for mushrooms, greens, and seasonings such as Sichuan peppercorns and fermented black beans. The fresh or frozen meat cases at Asian markets are usually stocked with thinly sliced meats. Alternatively, ask your butcher to slice the meat for you, or partially freeze the meat and then thinly slice it yourself with a chef's knife (see page 99).

A flavorful, rich broth is necessary for the best results. You can make you own chicken or beef stock (see pages 96 and 97), or you can purchase a high-quality low-sodium prepared broth at your local market.

cooking & serving

Broth fondues are typically consumed in two stages: First, individual pieces of meat, poultry, seafood, or vegetable are cooked in the simmering broth and eaten with a flavorful dipping sauce. Then whatever ingredients remain in the pot are ladled out along with the broth and served as a soup. Include the following items at each place setting: a shallow soup plate, chopsticks or a fondue fork, a soup spoon, and a table fork. Long-handled wire-mesh baskets or small tongs, available in Asian markets, can also be used to hold the foods in the simmering broth and retrieve them with ease. Put little dishes for dipping sauces and condiments near each place setting. Finally, have a ladle ready for serving the soup after all the foods have been cooked.

When you are ready to begin serving, pour the broth into the pot, filling it no more than three-quarters full. Turn the heat to at least 212°F on an electric pot, or light the fuel source, and bring the broth to a boil. Adjust the heat so the broth will remain at a steady simmer throughout the cooking.

Invite diners to pick up a piece of food from the communal platter with their chopsticks and immerse it in the simmering broth. If serving thinly sliced meat and using fondue forks, suggest threading the meat onto the fork accordion fashion (see page 99). The timing will depend on what you are cooking,

make ahead...

The long list of ingredients for broth fondues can seem daunting, but many of the elements can be prepared in advance: dipping sauces can be refrigerated overnight; meats, seafood, and vegetables can be arranged on platters and chilled for up to 2 hours before serving.

with thinly sliced beef taking no more than 45 seconds and chicken up to about 2 minutes. Once diners pull their cooked morsels from the hot broth, they should swirl them in the dipping sauce and then immediately eat them. In some cases, ingredients already in the pot can be fished out and eaten with the dipping sauce.

If the liquid reduces too much during cooking, stir in 1 to 2 cups additional hot broth or water. Some recipes call for adding noodles or other ingredients to the broth before serving it as a soup. Once they are heated through, ladle the soup into bowls and invite diners to season their servings with the remaining dipping sauce or other condiments.

sichuan hot pot

fermented black beans, 3 tbsp, rinsed

Chinese rice wine, ¼ cup plus 1 tbsp

whole green onions, 3 or 4, minced

fresh ginger, 2 tbsp minced

canola oil, 1 tbsp

purchased chile-garlic sauce, 1 tbsp or to taste

Chicken Stock (page 96) or reduced-sodium chicken broth, 6 cups

Chinese black vinegar or red wine vinegar, 1 tbsp

sugar, 1 tbsp

Sichuan peppercorns, 1 tbsp crushed

chicken breast, ½ lb, thinly sliced

pork tenderloin, ½ lb, thinly sliced

Garlic-Soy Dipping Sauce (page 96)

assorted fresh vegetables such as snow peas, baby bok choy, napa cabbage, or watercress leaves, 4–5 cups, cut into bite-sized pieces

firm tofu, 8–10 oz, cut into 1-inch cubes

assorted sliced fresh mushrooms such as shiitake, enoki, or cremini, 4 cups

bean thread noodles, 3 oz, soaked in hot water for 30 minutes and drained

Mash the black beans with the 1 tablespoon rice wine. In a large saucepan over medium heat, sauté the green onions and ginger in the oil until softened, 2–3 minutes. Add the black bean mixture and chile-garlic sauce and cook for 1 minute longer. Add the stock, the remaining ¼ cup rice wine, the vinegar, sugar, and crushed peppercorns and bring to a boil. Reduce the heat and simmer for 15 minutes.

Arrange the chicken and pork slices on a platter. Assemble an electric hot pot or skillet in the center of the table. Divide the dipping sauce among 4 individual bowls and set 1 at each place setting. Carefully transfer the stock mixture to the pot, adjusting the heat to keep it at a simmer. Add half each of the vegetables, tofu, and mushrooms and cook for 5 minutes.

Instruct diners to do the following: Cook a slice of chicken or pork in the broth until no longer pink, about 45 seconds (see page 57). Eat the meat with the dipping sauce, accompanied by pieces of vegetables, tofu, and mushrooms from the pot. After half of the meat has been eaten, add the remaining vegetables, tofu, and mushrooms to the broth and simmer for 5 minutes before the cooking the remaining meats.

Once all the meat has been cooked, compose the soup: Add the bean thread noodles to the pot and heat through for 2–3 minutes. Divide the soup among 4 bowls and serve right away.

SERVES 4

mongolian hot pot

Sesame-Soy Dipping Sauce (page 96)

lean lamb, 1¼ lb, cut into paper-thin slices

napa cabbage, 6 or 7 large leaves, cut into 2-inch squares

baby bok choy, 6 oz, cut into 2-inch pieces

green onions, 5, cut on the diagonal into ½-inch pieces, plus 5 green onions, finely chopped

red bell pepper, 1, stemmed, seeded, and cut into bite-sized pieces

dried shiitake mushrooms, 4, soaked in hot water for 30 minutes and drained, soaking liquid reserved

Beef or Chicken Stock (pages 96–97) or reduced-sodium beef or chicken broth, 6 cups

soy sauce, 2 tbsp

star anise, 1

fresh ginger, 1 tbsp finely chopped

firm tofu, 8–10 oz, cut into 1-inch cubes

bean sprouts, 1 cup

cremini mushrooms, 6–8, stemmed and cut into ¼-inch slices

bean thread noodles or rice vermicelli, 3 oz, soaked in hot water for 30 minutes and drained

Reserve ¼ cup of the dipping sauce and divide the rest among 4 individual bowls; set 1 bowl at each place setting. Arrange the lamb slices on a large rimmed platter and drizzle with the reserved sauce. Let stand for 20–30 minutes. Meanwhile, arrange the cabbage, bok choy, green onion pieces, and bell pepper on another platter. Remove and discard the stems from the shiitake mushrooms and cut the mushrooms into ¼-inch slices.

Assemble an electric hot pot or skillet in the center of the table. Add the stock, soy sauce, reserved mushroom liquid, star anise, ginger, chopped green onions, and sliced soaked shiitake mushrooms. Adjust the heat source to bring the broth to a boil, then reduce the heat and simmer for 20 minutes.

When ready to serve, add the tofu, bean sprouts, and cremini mushrooms to the broth. Instruct diners to do the following: Cook a piece of lamb, cabbage, bok choy, green onion, or bell pepper in the hot broth until cooked, about 1 minute (see page 57), and then eat with the dipping sauce.

Once all the lamb and vegetables have been cooked, compose the soup: Add the bean thread noodles to the broth and heat through for 2–3 minutes. Divide the soup among 4 bowls and serve right away with the remaining dipping sauce for seasoning.

SERVES 4

beef tenderloin or top-sirloin steak,
1 lb, cut into paper-thin slices

Pickled Onions (page 92)

Asian sesame oil, 2 tsp

Freshly ground pepper

butter lettuce, 1 large head,
leaves separated

fresh mint leaves, cilantro leaves,
and basil leaves, torn, 1 cup *each*

English cucumber, 1, peeled, halved
lengthwise, seeded, and thinly
sliced crosswise

fresh bean sprouts, 1½–2 cups

canola oil, 1 tbsp

garlic, 3 cloves, minced

lemongrass, tender inner parts only,
2 tbsp chopped

fresh ginger, 6 thin slices

tomato paste, 1 tbsp

white vinegar, ¼ cup

sugar, 1 tbsp

kosher salt, ½ tsp

Pineapple-Chile Salsa (page 93)

green onions, 2, cut on the diagonal
into thin slices

Arrange the beef slices on a platter and scatter the Pickled Onions over the top. Drizzle the beef and onions with the sesame oil and sprinkle lightly with pepper. Arrange the lettuce leaves on a platter along with the herbs, cucumber, and bean sprouts.

In a large saucepan over medium heat, warm the canola oil. Add the garlic, lemongrass, and ginger and sauté until fragrant, about 2 minutes. Add the tomato paste, vinegar, 2 cups water, the sugar, and salt and bring to a boil.

Assemble an electric hot pot or skillet in the center of the table. Set a small bowl of the Pineapple-Chile Salsa at each place setting. Carefully transfer the lemongrass broth to the pot, add the green onions, and adjust the heat source to keep the liquid at a simmer.

Instruct diners to do the following: Cook the beef and onions in the hot broth until the beef is no longer pink, about 45 seconds (see page 57). Then, transfer the cooked beef and onions to a piece of lettuce on a plate. Top with some of the herbs, cucumber slices, bean sprouts, and a dollop of the pineapple salsa. Roll up the fillings in the lettuce and pick up with your hands to enjoy.

SERVES 4

shabu-shabu

dried udon noodles, 5 oz, broken into 3-inch pieces

Herbed Ponzu Dipping Sauce (page 96)

well-marbled rib-eye or top-sirloin steak, 1 lb, very thinly sliced

napa cabbage, 5 or 6 leaves, cut into 2-inch squares

baby arugula, 1–2 cups lightly packed

green onions, 8–10, including tender green parts, cut on the diagonal into 1½- to 2-inch pieces

Chicken Stock (page 96) or reduced-sodium chicken broth, 3 cups

kombu, 1 sheet

enoki mushrooms, 1 bunch

fresh shiitake mushrooms, 8–10, stemmed and cut into ¼-inch slices

cremini mushrooms, 8–10, trimmed and cut into ¼-inch slices

wood-ear mushrooms, 5, halved (optional)

daikon, ¼ cup very thinly sliced (optional)

large carrot, 1, very thinly sliced

firm tofu, 8–10 oz, cut into 1-inch cubes

Sambal oelek, **hot chile oil,** and **chopped pickled ginger** for seasoning

Cook the noodles according to the package directions, drain, and set aside in a bowl of cold water. Divide the Herbed Ponzu Dipping Sauce among 4 individual dipping bowls and set 1 at each place setting.

Arrange the steak slices and half each of the cabbage, arugula, and green onions on 2 platters.

Assemble an electric hot pot or skillet in the center of the table. Pour the stock and 3 cups water into the pot and add the kombu. Adjust the heat to bring the broth just to a boil, and then immediately remove and discard the kombu. Add all of the mushrooms, the daikon (if using), and carrot to the pot and let simmer over low heat for 2–3 minutes. Add the tofu and the remaining cabbage, arugula, and green onions to the pot.

Instruct diners to do the following: Cook the steak and vegetables in the hot broth until cooked, 15–20 seconds (see page 57), then transfer to a shallow soup bowl and eat with the dipping sauce. Pass the seasonings at the table to flavor the dipping sauce.

About 10 minutes before all the steak and vegetables have been cooked, compose the soup: Drain the noodles, then add them to the broth and heat through for 2–3 minutes. Divide the soup among 4 bowls and serve right away with the remaining dipping sauce and seasonings.

SERVES 4

chicken fondue with romesco sauce

Chicken Stock (page 96) or reduced-sodium chicken broth, 6 cups

kosher salt, 1 tsp

carrots, 2, cut into ½-inch lengths

celery, 2 small stalks, cut into ½-inch lengths

leek, 1, white part only, halved lengthwise and cut into ¼-inch slices

green beans, 8–10, trimmed and cut into ½-inch pieces

dry vermouth, ½ cup plus 2 tbsp

Dijon mustard, 2 tbsp

fresh tarragon, 2 tbsp chopped

Freshly ground pepper

boneless, skinless chicken breasts, 1¼ lb, halved and cut on the diagonal into ¼-inch slices

zucchini, 1 small, trimmed, quartered lengthwise, and cut into ¼-inch slices

yellow squash, 1 small, trimmed, quartered lengthwise, and cut into ¼-inch slices

frozen peas, 1 cup

fresh flat-leaf parsley, 1 tbsp chopped

chives, 1 tbsp chopped

Romesco Sauce (page 94)

warm cooked long-grain rice, 3–4 cups

Pour the stock into a large saucepan and bring to a boil over high heat. Add the salt, carrots, celery, leek, and green beans, reduce the heat to medium, and simmer until the vegetables are tender-crisp, about 10 minutes. Using a slotted spoon, transfer the vegetables to a shallow dish and set aside. Raise the heat to high, bring the broth back to a boil, add the ½ cup vermouth, and cook until the liquid is reduced to about 4 cups, 12–15 minutes.

Meanwhile, in a small bowl, whisk together the remaining 2 tablespoons vermouth, the mustard, 1 tablespoon of the tarragon, and pepper to taste. Arrange the chicken slices on a platter and spread the mustard mixture on both sides of the slices. Let stand at room temperature for 15 minutes.

Assemble an electric hot pot or skillet in the center of the table. Carefully transfer the broth to the pot and adjust the heat to keep the broth at a simmer. Add the zucchini, squash, peas, parsley, chives, reserved cooked vegetables, and the remaining 1 tablespoon tarragon.

Instruct diners to do the following: Cook the chicken in the hot broth until no longer pink, 1–2 minutes (see page 57), and eat with the Romesco Sauce. After all the chicken has been cooked, compose the soup: Divide the rice among 4 soup bowls. Ladle some of the hot broth and vegetables over the rice and pass the remaining romesco for stirring into the soup.

SERVES 4

thai curry hot pot with seafood

rice stick noodles, 5 oz, broken into 3-inch pieces

Chicken Stock (page 96) or reduced-sodium chicken broth, 4 cups

lemongrass, 1 or 2 stalks, tender inner parts only, sliced or chopped

garlic, 2 cloves, chopped

fresh ginger, 2 slices, each ¼ inch thick, coarsely chopped

cilantro stems, 2 tbsp chopped

fish sauce, such as *nuoc mam*, ¼ cup

Thai green curry paste, 1–2 tbsp

lime, 1, zest finely grated and juiced

Kosher salt

unsweetened coconut milk, 1 can (13½ oz)

mixed fresh herbs such as cilantro, basil, and mint, 1 cup chopped

fresh shiitake mushrooms, ½ lb, stemmed and cut into ¼-inch slices

napa cabbage, ½ head, leaves separated and cut into 2-inch pieces

snow peas, ½ lb, stemmed and cut on the diagonal into 2 or 3 pieces

large shrimp, ¾ lb, peeled and deveined

firm-fleshed white fish such as halibut or cod, ¾ lb, cut into ¾-inch cubes

fresh squid, 4 or 5, cleaned, body cut into ½-inch rings and tentacles cut into 1-inch pieces

In a heatproof bowl, cover the noodles with hot water and let stand for 30 minutes. Drain and set aside.

In a large pot over medium-high heat, combine the stock, 3 cups water, the lemongrass, garlic, ginger, and cilantro stems and bring to a boil. Reduce the heat and simmer for 20 minutes. Strain the broth through a fine-mesh sieve set over a large bowl and discard the solids.

Assemble an electric hot pot or skillet in the center of the table. Carefully transfer the broth to the pot and add the fish sauce, 1 tablespoon of the curry paste, and the lime zest and juice. Adjust the heat to bring the broth to a simmer.

When ready to serve, stir the coconut milk into the broth and add the herbs, mushrooms, cabbage, and snow peas. Pat the shrimp, fish, and squid dry with paper towels, then arrange on a platter.

Instruct diners to do the following: Cook a piece of seafood or fish in the hot broth until opaque throughout, about 45 seconds (see page 57), then transfer, with a selection of vegetables, to a shallow bowl to eat. After about half the seafood and fish have been cooked, compose the soup: Add the remaining seafood and fish to the broth. Divide the reserved noodles among the bowls and ladle some of the soup over the top. Serve right away.

SERVES 4

about sweet fondues 70

bittersweet chocolate fondue 73

bourbon-caramel fondue 74

toasted coconut & white chocolate fondue with rum 77

mascarpone–vanilla bean fondue 78

swiss-style chocolate fondue 79

mexican chocolate fondue with orange essence 80

chile-spiced chèvre & brown sugar fondue 83

dulce de leche fondue 84

peanut butter & chocolate fondue 85

white chocolate–espresso fondue 86

sweet fondues

about sweet fondues

Sweet fondues are among the easiest fondues to make. Strawberries dipped into molten dark chocolate is perhaps the most popular of these communal desserts, but this chapter shows that many other delicious possibilities exist, from espresso-laced white chocolate and bourbon-spiked caramel to chile-spiced chèvre—all with inspired dippers to match.

equipment

Fondue pots specifically designed for dessert fondues are generally smaller and deeper than pots for cheese fondues and are typically made of heatproof ceramic, stainless steel, or enameled cast iron. Two-part stainless- steel pots with ceramic inserts also work well because their double boiler–like construction insulates heat-sensitive ingredients, such as chocolate, from direct contact with the heat source. A small electric fondue pot outfitted with a thermostat is a good choice, too, and allows you to make the fondue from start to finish at the table.

Sweet fondues can also be prepared and served without a fondue pot. Heat the chocolate or other ingredients in a double boiler over simmering water and then transfer the mixture to a warmed large communal dish or individual heatproof bowls or ramekins. Place the dish(es) on a raised trivet over a tea light to keep the fondue warm.

choosing dippers...

When choosing dippers to pair with dessert fondues, consider the sweetness of both the fondue and the dipper. In general, the dipper should not be as sweet as the fondue or the pairing will be overly sweet.

Fondue forks, cocktail forks, or small skewers are all suitable for immersing dippers into sweet fondues. Just make sure that whatever you choose is long enough so guests won't have to reach too deeply into the pot.

ingredients

The success of chocolate-based fondues hinges on the quality of the chocolate, so buy the best you can find. When shopping for bittersweet chocolate, look for a product with at least 70 percent chocolate liquor. Other common ingredients include white chocolate, soft cheeses, coconut milk, pure vanilla extract, and fresh cream, milk, and butter. Many of the following recipes call for bourbon, kirsch, Cognac, or other spirits, but an equal amount of fresh orange juice can be substituted for an alcohol-free dessert.

The recipes in this chapter are versatile. You can serve them year-round by simply varying the fruits or other dippers to suit the season. Angel food cake, pound cake, or thin butter cookies are delicious with almost any sweet fondue. If you have time, you can make your own dippers from scratch. Turn to pages 88 through 91 for a few creative recipes to get you started.

cooking & serving

Always chop or grate the ingredients for sweet fondues into small pieces so they will melt evenly, and never heat cream or milk to a boil, as you do not want a skin to form. Other than those two precautions, making sweet fondues is usually as simple as stirring the ingredients together over gentle heat until smooth.

Instruct guests to spear a dipper onto a fondue fork or other implement, dip it into

fondue party...

Put together a sweet fondue buffet the next time you entertain: Offer one chocolate, one caramel, and one sweet cheese fondue on a sideboard. Nearby, assemble a variety of dippers from which everyone can choose. Outfit guests with small plates, cocktail napkins, and small fondue forks, skewers, or cocktail picks.

the fondue, and then enjoy it right away. You can dispense with forks for larger items, such as Sugar Twists (page 89) or Churros (page 90), advising guests to dip only once if using a communal pot to avoid the taboo act of "double-dipping." If the fondue becomes too thick, stir in a little more cream or milk.

Dessert fondues don't have to be served hot. They need only to remain liquid enough for dipping. And if a few spoonfuls of fondue are left at the end of the evening, cover and refrigerate them. The next day, gently reheat them over warm water or in a microwave to yield a delicious sauce for drizzling over ice cream.

bittersweet chocolate fondue

bittersweet chocolate, ½ lb, coarsely chopped

heavy cream, ½ cup

framboise, kirsch, or Cognac, 2 tbsp

Kosher salt, pinch

Accompaniments of your choice (below)

goes great with...

- Sugar Twists, page 89, or purchased
- strawberries
- dried pear, peach, apricot, or mango slices
- pound cake, croissant, or angel food cake pieces
- ladyfingers

In a small fondue pot over very low heat, or in a double boiler over simmering water, combine the chocolate and cream and cook, stirring frequently, until the chocolate has completely melted. Add the framboise and salt and stir to combine.

Before serving, make sure the heat source under the fondue pot is set to very low just to keep the chocolate warm. Or, if making in a double boiler, transfer the warm chocolate mixture to a flameproof serving dish set on a raised trivet over tea lights. Serve right away with fondue forks and the accompaniments for dipping.

SERVES 4-6

bourbon-caramel fondue

sugar, 1½ cups

unsalted butter, 6 tbsp, cut into 6–8 pieces

heavy cream, 1¼ cups

bourbon, 3 tbsp

pure vanilla extract, 1 tsp

Accompaniments of your choice (below)

goes great with...

- marshmallows
- crisp waffle pieces
- biscotti
- apple or pear wedges
- banana slices
- shortbread
- toasted brioche or panettone cubes

In a saucepan over medium heat, combine ⅓ cup water and the sugar. Cook, swirling the pan 2 or 3 times but not stirring, until the sugar dissolves. Once the sugar has dissolved, cover the pan and cook, swirling once or twice, until the sugar turns to a light brown caramel and is thick and bubbling, 8–10 minutes. Uncover the pan and continue cooking the caramel until it turns golden brown, 3–4 minutes longer. Watch the caramel carefully; it turns brown very quickly. Remove the pan from the heat.

Stand back and carefully stir the butter into the caramel; it will foam vigorously and is very hot. When the foam has subsided, after a few seconds, add the heavy cream. Return the pan to low heat and cook, stirring carefully and scraping up any clumps on the bottom of the pan, until the mixture is smooth. Remove from the heat, add the bourbon and vanilla, and stir to combine.

Assemble a fondue pot in the center of the table. Light the fuel burner according to the manufacturer's instructions. Carefully pour the fondue into the fondue pot, using a heatproof silicone spatula to scrape clean the bottom and sides of the pot; keep warm over low heat. (If not using a fondue pot, transfer the fondue to a warmed flameproof serving dish set on a raised trivet over tea lights.) Serve right away with fondue forks and the accompaniments for dipping.

SERVES 4-6

toasted coconut & white chocolate fondue with rum

unsweetened coconut milk, ¼ cup plus 1–2 tbsp as needed

white chocolate, ¾ lb, finely chopped, or 1 package (¾ lb) white chocolate chips

lime zest, freshly grated from 1 lime

fresh lime juice, 2 tbsp

dark rum, 1 tbsp

kosher salt, pinch

flaked sweetened coconut, ½ cup, toasted in a 350°F oven for 8–10 mintues

Accompaniments of your choice (below)

goes great with...

- Sweet Crêpes, page 91, or purchased
- pineapple chunks
- kiwi slices
- strawberries
- banana slices
- toasted pound cake cubes
- crisp butter cookies

In a small fondue pot over very low heat, or in a double boiler over simmering water, combine the ¼ cup coconut milk and the white chocolate chips and cook over low heat, stirring constantly, until the chocolate is melted and the mixture is hot to the touch. Add the lime zest and juice, rum, and salt and stir to combine. Stir in the toasted coconut. If the mixture is too thick, stir in the 1–2 tablespoons coconut milk as needed to create a good dipping consistency.

Before serving, make sure the heat source under the fondue pot is set to very low just to keep the fondue warm. Or, if making in a double boiler, transfer the hot coconut-chocolate mixture to a flameproof serving dish set on a raised trivet over tea lights. Serve right away with fondue forks and the accompaniments for dipping.

SERVES 4-6

mascarpone-vanilla bean fondue

heavy cream, ½ cup

vanilla bean, 1

cornstarch, 2 tbsp

pure maple syrup, ⅓ cup

mascarpone cheese, 1 cup

fresh lemon juice, 2 tsp

kosher salt, pinch

Accompaniments of your choice (below)

goes great with...

- strawberries
- mandarin orange segments
- fresh or dried apricots and peaches
- lemon pound cake or angel food cake pieces
- ladyfingers

In a small saucepan over low heat, warm the heavy cream until hot to the touch, then remove from the heat. Using a small knife, cut the vanilla bean in half lengthwise and scrape out the vanilla seeds. Add the seeds and vanilla bean pod to the cream and let steep for 10–15 minutes. Remove the vanilla bean, rinse, let dry on paper towels, and reserve for another use. In a small bowl, combine the cornstarch and maple syrup and stir to dissolve.

About 10 minutes before serving, pour the vanilla-cream mixture into a fondue pot and warm over low heat. Add the mascarpone cheese and stir to combine. Stir in the maple syrup mixture and simmer, stirring frequently, until the fondue thickens, 3–4 minutes. Stir in the lemon juice and salt. (If not using a fondue pot, finish making the fondue in the saucepan on the stove top and transfer to a warmed flameproof serving dish set on a trivet over tea lights.) Serve right away with fondue forks and the accompaniments for dipping.

SERVES 4-6

milk chocolate candy bar with almond nougat, such as Toblerone, 3 bars (3½ oz each), coarsely chopped

heavy cream, ⅓ cup

honey, 2 tbsp

Cognac, 2 tbsp

kosher salt, pinch

Accompaniments of your choice (below)

goes great with...

- strawberries
- raspberries
- banana slices
- pound cake or angel food cake pieces
- ladyfingers
- Sugar Twists, page 89, or purchased

In a small fondue pot over very low heat, or in a double boiler over simmering water, combine the chocolate and cream and cook, stirring frequently, until the mixture is creamy and the chocolate has completely melted. Add the honey, Cognac, and salt and stir to combine.

Before serving, make sure the heat source under the fondue pot is set to very low just to keep the chocolate warm. Or, if making in a double boiler, transfer the warm chocolate mixture to a flameproof serving dish set on a raised trivet over tea lights. Serve right away with fondue forks and the accompaniments for dipping.

SERVES 4-6

mexican chocolate fondue
with orange essence

Mexican chocolate, 2 tablets (about 3 oz each), coarsely chopped

milk chocolate, 2 oz, coarsely chopped

heavy cream, ¼ cup, plus 1–2 tbsp as needed

pure vanilla extract, ½ tsp

ground cinnamon, 1 tsp

kosher salt, pinch

cayenne pepper, pinch

Triple Sec or Grand Marnier, 2 tbsp

Accompaniments of your choice (below)

goes great with...

- mandarin orange segments
- Churros, page 90, or purchased
- strawberries
- banana slices
- Cinnamon-Sugar Tortilla Chips, page 88
- toasted pound cake pieces

In a small fondue pot over very low heat, or in a double boiler over simmering water, combine the Mexican and milk chocolates and the cream and cook, stirring frequently, until the mixture is creamy and the chocolate has completely melted. Add the vanilla, cinnamon, salt, cayenne, and Triple Sec and stir to combine. If the mixture is too thick, stir in the 1–2 tablespoons cream as needed to create a good dipping consistency.

Before serving, make sure the heat source under the fondue pot is set to very low just to keep the chocolate warm. Or, if making in a double boiler, transfer the hot chocolate mixture to a flameproof serving dish set on a raised trivet over tea lights. Serve right away with fondue forks and the accompaniments for dipping.

SERVES 4

chile-spiced chèvre & brown sugar fondue

creamy goat cheese (chèvre), ½ lb,
cut into ½-inch slices

cream sherry, ¼ cup

whole milk or half-and-half, ¼ cup
plus 1–2 tbsp

dark brown sugar, ¼ cup firmly
packed

pure vanilla extract, 1 tsp

ancho chile powder, 1 tbsp

ground cinnamon, ½ tsp

kosher salt, pinch

**Accompaniments of your choice
(below)**

In a small fondue pot over very low heat, or in a double boiler over simmering water, combine the goat cheese, sherry, the ¼ cup milk, brown sugar, vanilla, chile powder, cinnamon, and salt and cook, stirring frequently, until the mixture is creamy and the cheese has completely melted. If the mixture is too thick, stir in the 1–2 tablespoons milk as needed to create a good dipping consistency.

Before serving, make sure the heat source under the fondue pot is set to very low just to keep the fondue warm. Or, if making in a double boiler, transfer the spiced cheese mixture to a flameproof serving dish set on a raised trivet over tea lights. Serve right away with fondue forks and the accompaniments for dipping.

SERVES 4-6

goes great with...

- Cinnamon-Sugar Tortilla Chips (page 88)
- dried fruit such as apricots, apples, and peaches
- toasted brioche or panettone cubes
- biscotti
- apple wedges
- strawberries

dulce de leche fondue

whole hazelnuts, 1/3 cup (about 2 oz)

dulce de leche, 1 can (about 13 1/2 oz)

half-and-half, 1/4–1/2 cup

Frangelico or amaretto liqueur, 2 tbsp

kosher salt, pinch

Accompaniments of your choice (below)

goes great with...

- pineapple chunks
- banana slices
- strawberries
- angel food cake pieces
- Sugar Twists, page 89, or purchased
- biscotti

In a small dry frying pan over medium heat, toast the hazelnuts until fragrant and golden, about 10 minutes. Transfer them to a kitchen towel and rub vigorously to remove the skins. Finely chop the hazelnuts and set aside.

In a small fondue pot over very low heat, or in a double boiler over simmering water, combine the *dulce de leche*, 1/4 cup of the half-and-half, the Frangelico, chopped hazelnuts, and salt and cook over low heat, stirring, until hot to the touch. If the mixture is too thick, stir in the remaining half-and-half as needed to create a good dipping consistency.

Before serving, make sure the heat source under the fondue pot is set to very low just to keep the fondue warm. Or, if making in a double boiler, transfer the hot *dulce de leche* mixture to a warmed fondue pot or flameproof serving dish set on a raised trivet over tea lights. Serve right away with fondue forks and the accompaniments for dipping.

SERVES 4-6

peanut butter & chocolate fondue

light corn syrup, ¼ cup

whole milk, ⅓ cup

Cognac or brandy, 2 tbsp

bittersweet chocolate, 6 oz,
coarsely chopped

smooth or chunky peanut butter,
½ cup

pure vanilla extract, 1 tsp

kosher salt, pinch

**Accompaniments of your choice
(below)**

goes great with...

- graham crackers
- pretzels
- banana slices
- mandarin orange segments
- crisp chocolate cookies

In a small fondue pot over very low heat, or in a double boiler over simmering water, combine the corn syrup, milk, and Cognac and cook until hot to the touch. Add the chopped chocolate and peanut butter and cook, stirring frequently, until the mixture is creamy and the chocolate has completely melted. Add the vanilla and salt and stir to combine.

Before serving, make sure the heat source under the fondue pot is set to very low just to keep the mixture warm. Or, if making in a double boiler, transfer the hot chocolate mixture to a flameproof serving dish set on a raised trivet over tea lights. Serve right away with fondue forks and the accompaniments for dipping.

SERVES 4-6

white chocolate-espresso fondue

half-and-half, ½ cup

instant espresso powder, 2 tsp

white chocolate, ¾ lb, finely chopped, or 1 package (¾ lb) white chocolate chips

coffee liqueur, 2 tbsp

kosher salt, pinch

Accompaniments of your choice (below)

goes great with...

- Caramel Corn Clusters, page 91, or purchased caramel kettle corn
- chocolate angel food cake pieces
- ladyfingers
- biscotti
- Sugar Twists, page 89, or purchased
- crystallized ginger slices
- dried apricots

In a small fondue pot over very low heat, or in a double boiler over simmering water, combine the half-and-half, espresso powder, and white chocolate and cook, stirring frequently, until the mixture is creamy and the chocolate has completely melted. Add the coffee liqueur and salt and stir to combine.

Before serving, make sure the heat source under the fondue pot is set to very low just to keep the mixture warm. Or, if making in a double boiler, transfer the hot chocolate mixture to a flameproof serving dish set on a raised trivet over tea lights. Serve right away with fondue forks and the accompaniments for dipping.

SERVES 4-6

homemade dippers

Below are some creative ideas for handmade dippers, which boast better flavor and a more elegant appeal than their store-bought counterparts. These items can be prepared in advance, making them excellent choices for entertaining. Whether serving a savory or sweet fondue, making at least one dipper from scratch will add flair to your table.

tortilla chips

Canola, safflower, or peanut oil

small corn tortillas, 8, each cut into 6 wedges

Kosher salt

Pour enough oil into a heavy-bottomed saucepan to reach $1/2$ inch up the sides of the pan. Warm the oil over medium-high heat until it reaches 350°F on a deep-frying thermometer. Carefully add the tortilla wedges to the oil and fry for 20 seconds. Using a slotted spoon, turn the wedges over and fry until pale golden, about 20 seconds longer. Lift the chips from the oil, transfer to a paper towel–lined plate to drain, and sprinkle with salt to taste. Store in an airtight container for up to 2 days. Makes 48 chips, 4–6 servings.

Variation: Cinnamon-Sugar Tortilla Chips
Follow the recipe to make Tortilla Chips, using flour tortillas in place of the corn tortillas. After draining, transfer the fried chips to a bowl, sprinkle with 2 tablespoons confectioners' sugar and $1/2$ teaspoon ground cinnamon instead of the salt, and toss well.

baked pita strips

pita breads, 2

Kosher salt

Preheat the oven to 350°F. Cut the pita breads in half, then cut each half crosswise into 6 strips. Transfer the strips to a baking sheet and bake until crisp and slightly browned, about 10 minutes. Remove from the oven and sprinkle with salt to taste. Makes 24 strips, 4–6 servings.

polenta cubes

Unsalted butter

Kosher salt

coarse yellow cornmeal, 1 cup

Butter an 8-by-8-inch baking pan. In a heavy saucepan over high heat, bring 5 cups water to a boil. Add a pinch of salt and whisk in the cornmeal, stirring constantly to prevent lumps from forming. Reduce the heat to low and simmer, stirring often, until the polenta pulls away from the sides of the pan but is still thin enough to fall from the whisk, about 30 minutes. Remove the pan from the heat. Pour the polenta into the prepared pan and spread into an even layer. Cover and refrigerate until firm, at least 2 hours or up to overnight.

Using a sharp knife, cut the firm polenta into 1-inch cubes and use a spatula to lift them from the pan. Makes 64 cubes.

caramelized shallot halves

shallots, 6 small

olive oil, 2 tsp

Kosher salt

Cut the shallots in half lengthwise, leaving the root ends intact, then peel the shallots. In a large sauté pan over medium-high heat, warm the oil until it shimmers. Add the shallot halves, cut side down, and cook until golden, 1–2 minutes. Turn the shallots over and cook for 1–2 minutes longer. Remove from the heat and sprinkle with salt to taste. Makes 12 shallot halves.

grilled apples

Granny Smith or other tart apples, 2, cored and cut into 8 wedges

Canola oil, 2 tbsp (optional)

sugar, 1 cup (optional)

Prepare a gas or charcoal grill for direct-heat grilling over medium-high heat.

If you are serving a savory fondue, brush the apple wedges with canola oil. If you are serving a sweet fondue, in a small saucepan over medium-high heat, cook the sugar with 2 tablespoons water until dissolved, about 5 minutes. Brush the apples with the sugar-water mixture.

Grill the apple slices for about 2 minutes on each side, until both sides have distinct, golden grill marks. Makes 16 wedges.

sugar twists

purchased frozen puff pastry, 1 sheet, thawed

sugar, 1 cup

Preheat the oven to 375°F. Line 2 baking sheets with parchment paper.

Carefully unfold the puff pastry (it's usually folded into thirds), then refold the pastry in half. Sprinkle ½ cup of the sugar evenly over a work surface and place the folded puff pastry on top. Sprinkle the remaining ½ cup sugar over the top of the pastry. Using a rolling pin, roll out the dough into a long rectangle about 9 inches wide, 24 inches long, and just under ¼ inch thick. You may need to sprinkle the sugar from the work surface onto and under the pastry so that it doesn't stick. Using a pastry wheel or sharp knife, trim the edges all around to form an even rectangle. Then, cut the pastry crosswise into strips ¾ inch wide and lay flat on another baking sheet. Place the strips in the freezer for about 10 minutes to chill.

Using both hands, pick up the dough strips from each end and twist several times. Arrange the finished twists on the prepared baking sheets, spacing them evenly. Bake until golden brown, about 15 minutes, turning the baking sheet halfway through baking. Transfer to a wire rack to cool completely. Store in an airtight container at room temperature for up to 1 day or freeze for up to 1 week. Makes 25–30 twists.

churros

sugar, 1 cup plus 2 tsp

ground cinnamon, 2 tsp

milk, 1 cup

unsalted butter, ¼ cup, cut into pieces

kosher salt, ½ tsp

all-purpose flour, 1 cup

large eggs, 4

canola oil, 3 cups

In a bowl, whisk together the 1 cup sugar and the cinnamon; set aside.

In a saucepan over medium-high heat, combine the milk, butter, the remaining 2 teaspoons sugar, and the salt. Bring to a boil, stirring occasionally, until the butter is melted. Add the flour all at once and beat vigorously with a wooden spoon until a shiny dough forms, about 1 minute. Transfer to a large bowl and let cool for 5 minutes. Using an electric mixer on medium-low speed, beat in the eggs, 1 at a time. Continue to beat until a shiny, sticky paste forms, about 2 minutes.

In a large, deep, heavy-bottomed saucepan, warm the oil until it registers 350°F on a deep-frying thermometer. Spoon the batter into a pastry bag fitted with a medium star tip.

Working in batches, pipe 4-inch-long ribbons of dough into the hot oil (use a knife if necessary to cut the batter from the tip). Fry the churros, using tongs to turn them once or twice, until golden brown and cooked through in the center, about 3 minutes total. Transfer the churros to paper towels to drain, then immediately toss them in the reserved cinnamon-sugar mixture to coat completely. Bring the oil back to 350°F before frying the next batch. Serve warm. Makes about 24 churros.

sweet crêpes

whole milk, ½ cup

large eggs, 2

all-purpose flour, 1 cup

sugar, 2 tsp

pure vanilla extract, 1 tsp

Canola oil

In a blender, combine ½ cup water, the milk, eggs, flour, sugar, and vanilla and blend until very smooth. Cover and refrigerate for at least 1 hour or up to 1 day.

Lightly brush a nonstick 9-inch frying pan with oil and place over medium heat. Pour 2–3 tablespoons of the batter into the pan and immediately swirl the pan to cover the bottom with batter. Cook until the crêpe begins to bubble and brown a little and looks set, about 1 minute. Using a small offset spatula, flip the crêpe and cook until the second side is lightly browned and set, about 10 seconds. Transfer the crêpe to a piece of waxed paper.

Repeat with the remaining batter, stacking the finished crêpes between pieces of waxed paper as you work. Makes 8 crêpes.

caramel corn clusters

sugar, ¾ cup

butter, 3 tbsp

heavy cream, ¾ cup

kosher salt, pinch

air-popped popcorn, 6 cups

Preheat the oven to 350°F. Line 2 rimmed baking sheets with parchment paper.

Spread the sugar evenly in a deep, heavy-bottomed saucepan. Warm over medium-high heat, without stirring, until it starts to melt around the edges. Continue to cook, stirring, until the sugar melts completely and turns a light amber, 2–3 minutes. Carefully whisk in the butter, cream, and salt until thoroughly mixed.

Remove the pan from the heat, and then gently stir in the popcorn until coated. Transfer the caramel corn to a lined baking sheet. Bake for 15–20 minutes to crisp. Remove from the oven and let stand for about 5 minutes.

Using a spoon and your hands, pull away clusters of caramel corn and shape slightly into balls. Set aside on the second lined baking sheet. Store in an airtight container for up to 1 day. Makes about 24 clusters.

sauces, accompaniments & stocks

Although each of the fondue recipes in this book is paired with a particular sauce or accompaniment, many of them are interchangeable, so you can mix and match to your own tastes. A high-quality homemade stock will add unmatched flavor to your broth-based fondues, so it's a good idea to keep some on hand in the freezer.

mushroom-herb paste

unsalted butter, 3 tbsp

cremini mushrooms, 1 lb, finely chopped

shallots, ¼ cup finely chopped

fresh thyme leaves, 1 tbsp

fresh tarragon leaves, 1 tbsp chopped

white wine vinegar, 2 tbsp

kosher salt, ½ tsp

freshly ground white pepper, ¼ tsp

In a large frying pan over medium-high heat, melt the butter. When the butter foams, add the mushrooms and shallots and sauté for 3–4 minutes. Add the thyme, tarragon, vinegar, salt, and pepper and continue to cook until no liquid remains in the bottom of the pan, 2–3 minutes. Transfer the mixture to a bowl to cool slightly. Makes 1½ cups.

pickled onions

yellow onion, 1 large

white vinegar, ½ cup

Peel and thinly slice the onion and transfer to a small bowl. Pour the vinegar over the onion slices and stir to coat. Let the onions marinate for about 5 minutes, then drain and set aside until ready to use. Makes 1½ cups.

mango relish

canola oil, 2 tbsp

white onion, 1 cup diced

jalapeño chile, 1, stemmed, seeded, and minced

fresh ginger, 2 tsp finely chopped

garlic, 1 clove, minced

frozen mango chunks, 1 lb, thawed and cut into ½-inch pieces

cider vinegar, ¼ cup

light brown sugar, ¼ cup firmly packed

golden raisins, 3 tbsp

orange, 1, zest finely grated

fresh orange juice, ½ cup

ground allspice, ½ tsp

dry mustard, ½ tsp

kosher salt, ½ tsp

Freshly ground pepper

In a large saucepan over medium heat, warm the canola oil. Add the onion, jalapeño, and ginger and sauté until softened, about 5 minutes. Add the garlic and cook for 1 minute. Add the mango chunks, vinegar, brown sugar, raisins, orange zest and juice, allspice, mustard, salt, and pepper to taste and bring to a boil. Reduce the heat to medium-low and simmer, stirring occasionally, until the liquid has reduced to a few tablespoons, about 20 minutes. Remove the relish from the heat and set aside until ready to serve. Serve warm or chilled. Makes 2½ cups.

pineapple-chile salsa

garlic, 2 cloves, chopped

fresh red chile, 1, stemmed, seeded, and chopped, or 2 dried red chiles

anchovy paste, 2 tsp

sugar, 2 tbsp

lime, 1, zest finely grated

fresh lime juice, 1½ tbsp

rice wine vinegar, 1–2 tsp

Vietnamese fish sauce (*nuoc mam*), 3 tbsp

fresh pineapple, 1 cup chopped

In a blender, pulse the garlic, chile, anchovy paste, sugar, lime zest and juice, vinegar, and fish sauce until finely chopped. Add the chopped pineapple and pulse until the ingredients are blended but still retain some texture. Transfer the salsa to a bowl, cover, and refrigerate for at least 2 hours or up to overnight. Bring to room temperature before serving. Makes 1 cup.

spicy peanut sauce

Chicken Stock (page 96) or reduced-sodium chicken broth, ⅔–¾ cup

chunky peanut butter, ⅓ cup

brown sugar, 1 tbsp firmly packed

soy sauce, 1 tbsp

cider vinegar, 2 tsp

chile sauce such as *sambal oelek*, ½ tsp, or ¼ tsp red pepper flakes

garlic, 1 large clove, minced

fresh ginger, ½ tsp finely grated

green onions, 2, white and pale green parts only, minced

Chopped fresh cilantro for garnish

In a small saucepan over medium-low heat, whisk together ⅔ cup of the stock, the peanut butter, brown sugar, soy sauce, vinegar, chile sauce, garlic, ginger, and green onions. Bring to a low simmer and cook, stirring occasionally, until the mixture is smooth and creamy, about 5 minutes. If the sauce is too thick, stir in the remaining ¼ cup stock. Cover and keep warm until ready to serve. Garnish with the cilantro just before serving. Makes 1 cup.

romesco sauce

extra-virgin olive oil, 2 tbsp

fresh bread crumbs, 3 tbsp

garlic, 3 cloves

slivered or sliced almonds, ½ cup

roasted red bell peppers, ¾ cup chopped

oil-packed sun-dried tomatoes, 4 large, slivered

Chicken Stock (page 96) or reduced-sodium chicken broth, ⅓ cup, plus more as needed

sherry vinegar, 2 tbsp

sweet paprika, preferably Spanish, 1 tbsp

kosher salt, ½ tsp

red pepper flakes, ¼ tsp

In a small frying pan over medium heat, warm the olive oil. Add the bread crumbs and cook, stirring occasionally, until golden, 3–4 minutes. Using a food processor with the motor running, drop the garlic and almonds through the feed tube to finely chop. Scrape down the sides of the work bowl and add the toasted bread crumbs, bell peppers, sun-dried tomatoes, stock, vinegar, paprika, salt, and red pepper flakes. Process until the mixture is well combined and fairly smooth. Taste and adjust the seasonings, adding more salt if needed. Transfer the sauce to a bowl, cover, and refrigerate for at least 2 hours or up to 2 days. Bring to room temperature before serving. The sauce may thicken as it stands. If needed, stir in 1–2 tablespoons stock or water to create a good dipping consistency. Makes 1¼ cups.

honey-mustard sauce

whole-grain mustard, ¼ cup

sour cream, ⅓ cup

honey, 1½ tbsp

In a small bowl, whisk together the mustard, sour cream, and honey. Cover and refrigerate until ready to serve. Makes about ½ cup.

creamy horseradish sauce

crème fraîche, ¾ cup

sour cream, ½ cup

prepared creamed horseradish, 2 tbsp

Dijon mustard, 2 tsp

kosher salt, ½ tsp

Freshly ground pepper

In a small bowl, whisk together the crème fraîche, sour cream, horseradish, mustard, salt, and freshly ground pepper to taste. Cover and refrigerate until ready to serve. Makes about 1¼ cups.

lemon-caper rémoulade

capers, 2 tbsp

mayonnaise, ⅔ cup

Dijon mustard, 1 tbsp

sweet pickle, 1 tbsp chopped

green onions, 2 tbsp minced, white and pale green parts only

fresh flat-leaf parsley, 1½ tbsp chopped

fresh tarragon, 1 tbsp chopped

anchovy paste, 1 tsp

sugar, ½ tsp

Freshly ground pepper

Drain the capers and then finely chop.

In a bowl, stir together the mayonnaise, mustard, chopped capers, pickle, green onions, parsley, tarragon, anchovy paste, sugar, and pepper to taste. Cover and refrigerate for at least 1 hour or up to 2 days. Makes 1 cup.

chipotle tartar sauce

mayonnaise, 1 cup

fresh lemon juice, 2 tbsp

sweet pickle, 2 tbsp chopped

fresh cilantro, 2 tbsp finely chopped

shallot, 1 tbsp minced

canned chipotle chile in adobo sauce, 1 tsp minced, plus ½ tsp adobo sauce

Dijon mustard, 1 tsp

In a bowl, combine the mayonnaise, lemon juice, pickle, cilantro, shallot, chipotle chile and adobo sauce, and mustard. Whisk until well blended. Cover and refrigerate for at least 1 hour or up to 2 days. Makes 1 cup.

wasabi dipping sauce

mayonnaise, ½ cup

prepared wasabi paste, 1 tsp

fresh lemon juice, 1½ tbsp

soy sauce, 1 tsp

sugar, 1 tsp

In a bowl, combine the mayonnaise, wasabi paste, lemon juice, soy sauce, and sugar. Whisk until well blended. Cover and refrigerate until ready to serve. Makes about ⅔ cup.

garlic-soy dipping sauce

soy sauce, ¼ cup

Chinese rice wine, ¼ cup

green onions, 2, minced

garlic, 2 cloves, minced

Asian sesame oil, 2 tsp

Chicken Stock (bottom right) or reduced-sodium chicken broth, ½ cup

Seasonings: hoisin sauce, chile-garlic sauce, soy sauce, oyster sauce

In a small bowl, whisk together the soy sauce, rice wine, green onions, garlic, sesame oil, and stock. Pass the seasonings at the table so guests can customize their sauce according to their taste. Makes about 1 cup.

sesame-soy dipping sauce

soy sauce, ½ cup

rice wine vinegar, ⅓ cup

Chicken Stock (right) or reduced-sodium chicken broth, ¼ cup

Asian sesame oil, 1 tsp

Seasonings: Chinese mustard powder mixed with equal parts water; hoisin sauce; hot chile oil; sriracha chile sauce; Thai sweet chile sauce

In a small bowl, whisk together the soy sauce, vinegar, stock, and sesame oil. Pass

the seasonings at the table so guests can customize their sauce according to their taste. Makes about 1 cup.

herbed ponzu dipping sauce

fresh lemon juice, 6 tbsp

soy sauce, 6 tbsp

fresh cilantro, 1 tsp minced

sugar, ½ tsp

garlic, 2 cloves, minced

In a bowl, stir together the lemon juice, soy sauce, 1 tablespoon water, the cilantro, sugar, and garlic. Let stand for about 10 minutes. Makes about ⅔ cup.

chicken stock

fresh flat-leaf parsley, 4 sprigs

fresh thyme, 1 sprig

bay leaf, 1

chicken necks and backs, 6 lb

celery stalks, 3

carrots, 3, peeled

onions, 2, root ends cut off, halved

leeks, 2, white and pale green parts only, sliced

Wrap the parsley, thyme, and bay leaf in a piece of cheesecloth and tie with kitchen string. Add the herb bundle, chicken parts, celery, carrots, onions, and leeks to a large stockpot. Add enough cold water to just cover the ingredients. Place the pot over medium heat and slowly bring to a boil. Reduce the heat to as low as possible and simmer for 3 hours. While the stock simmers, use a spoon or skimmer to skim off the foam that rises to the surface.

Strain the stock through a cheesecloth-lined strainer into a large heatproof bowl. Let cool to room temperature, then cover and refrigerate overnight. Using a large spoon, remove the hardened fat from the surface and discard. Cover and refrigerate the stock for up to 3 days, or pour into airtight containers and freeze for up to 3 months. Makes 3 quarts.

beef stock

beef bones with some meat attached, 4 lb

fresh flat-leaf parsley, 4 sprigs

fresh thyme, 1 sprig

bay leaf, 1

large carrots, 2, cut into 2-inch slices

large onion, 1, cut into 2-inch slices

leeks, 2, pale and dark green parts only, sliced into 2-inch chunks

Preheat the oven to 425°F. Place the beef bones in a large roasting pan and roast, stirring occasionally, until the meat and bones are well browned, about $1\frac{1}{2}$ hours. Meanwhile, wrap the parsley, thyme, and bay leaf in a piece of cheesecloth and tie with kitchen string.

Remove the pan from the oven and place on the stove top over 2 burners. Transfer the bones to a large stockpot. Add the carrots, onion, leeks, and the herb bundle to the pot. Add about 3 cups water to the roasting pan and bring to a boil over medium-high heat, using a wooden spoon to scrape up the browned bits on the pan bottom. Pour the juices into the stockpot.

Add enough cold water to just cover the ingredients. Place the pot over medium heat and slowly bring the stock to a boil. Reduce the heat to low and simmer for 4 hours. While the stock simmers, use a spoon or skimmer to skim off the foam that rises to the surface. Strain the stock through a cheesecloth-lined strainer into a heatproof bowl. Let cool, then cover and refrigerate overnight. Using a large spoon, remove the hardened fat from the surface of the stock and discard. Cover the stock and refrigerate for up to 3 days, or pour into airtight containers and freeze for up to 3 months. Makes 3 quarts.

cutting bread into cubes

Nothing beats cubes of crusty bread dipped in creamy cheese fondue. Rustic, artisanal Italian breads and French baguettes work best for fondue because their sturdy texture and thick crusts hold the bread cubes together when dipped. You can also toast the bread cubes in a 350°F oven until lightly golden, about 5 minutes, before serving.

cut into slices

Holding the bread securely on the board with one hand, use a serrated bread knife to cut the bread crosswise into slices about 1 inch thick.

cut into strips

Cut the slices lengthwise into strips about 1 inch wide. Depending on the width of the bread, you may have to make a few cuts.

cut into cubes

Cut the strips crosswise to make 1-inch cubes. Cutting the bread this way ensures that each piece has some crust to help hold it together on the fondue fork.

working with meat

When cooking meat from its raw state in broth, it's important to slice it very thinly. This ensures that your guests won't need to hold their fondue fork in the pot for several minutes waiting for the meat to cook, and it keeps the flow of the evening at a good pace. Freezing the meat for about an hour before slicing makes the task much easier.

trim the fat

Using a sharp chef's knife, trim away as much external fat from the partially frozen meat as possible. The internal fat in meat, called "marbling," is fine and will add flavor.

slice the meat

With one hand, hold the meat securely on a cutting board. Using a gentle sawing motion, cut the meat across the grain into paper-thin slices, or as called for in the recipe.

secure the meat

To make sure the meat is secured onto the fondue fork or skewer, fold it back and forth a few times, creating an "S" fold, also called an accordion fold, then insert the prongs of the fork through the center of the folds.

blanching vegetables

Partially cooking vegetables in boiling water, or *blanching* them, makes them more appealing to eat. There are three things to keep in mind when blanching: First, be sure the vegetables are of similar size so they cook evenly. Next, remove the vegetables from the water as soon as they are done. Finally, chill the vegetables quickly to stop the cooking.

boil briefly

Fill a large saucepan three-fourths full of water and bring to a boil. Add a large pinch of salt, followed by the vegetables, and let cook for a few minutes.

lift from the water

As soon as the vegetables are vibrant and tender-crisp (taste a piece), use a skimmer or slotted spoon to remove them from the water. The timing will vary: thick asparagus spears may take 5 minutes to cook while sugar snap peas only need about 2 minutes.

cool in an ice bath

Immediately transfer the blanched vegetables to a large bowl filled with water and ice. This "shocks" the vegetables, or stops their cooking, and it also keeps their color vibrant. After a minute or two, drain the vegetables and let them come to room temperature

working with potatoes

The best potatoes to use for fondue dippers are small varieties such as red potatoes, fingerlings, or small Yukon gold potatoes. Using small potatoes allows you to cut bite-sized pieces that will have some skin on each piece, which helps keep the potato from falling apart when dipped, and prevents the vegetable from slipping off the fork.

cook the potatoes

Put the potatoes in a saucepan and add water to cover. Bring to a boil over high heat, then reduce the heat to medium and cook just until the potatoes are tender, 10–20 minutes, depending on the size of the potatoes.

test for doneness

Use a pair of tongs to pull a potato out of the water and insert a paring knife into the center. It is done when the knife just slips easily into the potato. Do not overcook the potatoes or they will fall apart or slip off the fork into the fondue pot.

cut into pieces

Drain the potatoes through a colander. Using a paring knife, halve the potatoes length-wise, then cut the two halves crosswise to make four equal-sized pieces; the pieces should be bite sized.

cutting bell-pepper squares

If you are using fondue forks or skewers, it is best to cut bell peppers into large squares so that they are easier to secure onto the fondue fork. The technique shown below helps create uniform squares that are relatively flat. If you wish to dip without using forks, cut the bell peppers into long, thin strips, instead of squares, in step 3.

trim the ends

Using a chef's knife, cut a thin slice from the top and bottom of the bell pepper and then stand the pepper on one of its ends on the cutting board.

remove the seeds

Cut through one side of the bell pepper from top to bottom, open it up, and lay it flat on the cutting board. Cut out and discard the ribs and seeds.

cut into squares

Depending on the size of the bell pepper, cut it lengthwise into 2–4 pieces so that each piece is relatively flat. Cut each piece into squares about 1 inch in size.

working with other ingredients

Fennel and pineapple are both delicious as fondue dippers, but their awkward shapes can be daunting to work with. Below you'll find some tips for working with each of them. Chocolate's dense yet slippery texture can make it difficult to cut. Following is a foolproof technique for cutting chocolate into fine, even pieces for smooth melting.

slicing fennel

Using a chef's knife, cut away the stalks from the bulb. Cut the bulb in half through the core. With the cut sides facing up, make a V-shaped cut in each half to remove the tough part of the core. Turn the halves cut sides down and cut lengthwise through the core into thin slices.

cubing pineapple

Using a chef's knife, cut off the top and bottom of the pineapple. Following the contour of the fruit, cut off the skin, then cut the fruit lengthwise into quarters. Cut the core from each quarter, then cut the fruit into rough, 1-inch cubes.

chopping chocolate

The teeth of a serrated knife work well to cut through all types of chocolate. With one hand gripping the handle of the knife and the other one on the top of the blade, push straight down to chop the chocolate block into small pieces. Aim for pieces that are about the same size to facilitate melting.

glossary

bean thread noodles Dried cellophane noodles made from the starch of mung beans, bean thread noodles are translucent when dry and turn transparent when they are soaked in water.

black beans, fermented Sometimes called preserved or salted black beans, fermented black beans are soybeans that have been dried, salted, and allowed to ferment until they turn black.

Calvados Apple cider aged in oak barrels, this dry apple brandy comes from northern France, where apples are plentiful. It is widely available at liquor stores.

cheese, blue Blue cheeses are inoculated with the spores of special molds to develop a network of blue veins for a sharp, peppery flavor that intensifies with age. Some of the most popular types include milder Gorgonzola and Maytag, as well as stronger blues such as Roquefort and Stilton.

cheese, Brie Ivory-colored Brie cheese is made from pasteurized or unpasteurized cow's milk. Many prefer the unpasteurized version, but it is rare outside of Europe. Brie is sold in flat rounds of various sizes. Its mild flavor, creamy texture, and buttery richness make it a delicious choice for fondue.

cheese, Camembert This soft, creamy cow's milk cheese originates from the French region of Normandy. Similiar to Brie, the cheese is sold in small rounds and has a soft white rind that needs to be removed before it is added to a fondue.

cheese, Edam A semi-hard cow's milk cheese from the Netherlands, this cheese is Gouda's cousin. It is a mild, all-purpose cheese made in part with skimmed milk. It pairs well with crisp apples, pears, and dark beer.

cheese, Emmentaler A cow's milk cheese produced in the mountains of Europe, mostly in Switzerland, Emmentaler is distinguished by its random holes. It is ivory in color and mildly nutty in flavor.

cheese, fontina A rich, semi-firm cow's-milk cheese with an earthy, mild flavor, the best fontina is from the Piedmont region of Italy. Varieties produced elsewhere lack the complex flavor of Italian fontina, but all types are excellent for melting.

cheese, fresh goat Also called *chèvre*, this pure white cheese is made from goat's milk. It has a tangy flavor and a soft, creamy texture. It is often sold in logs, but can also be found in small disks and cone shapes.

cheese, Gruyère A firm, nutty cow's milk cheese, Gruyère is a Swiss cheese, although it is also produced in France. It is a good melting cheese and has a more assertive flavor than some other cheeses commonly used in fondues.

cheese, Havarti A semi-hard Danish cow's milk cheese, Havarti is rindless and melts easily, making it a natural choice for fondue. It pairs well with dried and fresh fruits, hearty bread, and wine.

cheese, Manchego A sheep's milk cheese made in the Spanish region of La Mancha, this cheese has a tangy, nutty flavor, firm texture, and an ivory to pale gold color. Its rind, which can range from yellow to greenish black, is covered with a braided pattern. Italian pecorino romano can be substituted.

cheese, Mascarpone This fresh Italian cheese is made from cream, is soft, rich, and smooth with a texture reminiscent of sour cream.

chile-garlic sauce Similar to *sambal oelek* (see page 107), this milder sauce is also made with chiles, salt, and sometimes vinegar, but has the addition of garlic.

chipotle chiles Ripe, red jalapeño chiles that have been dried and smoked, chipotle chiles can be found whole and dried, in powder form, and canned in a spicy chile sauce called *adobo*.

chocolate, bittersweet Bittersweet chocolate contains anywhere from 35 to 70 percent chocolate liquor. When choosing chocolate

for fondue, look for a brand with 70 percent liquor. High-quality brands include Valrhona, Callebaut and Scharffen Berger.

chocolate, Mexican Commonly used for making hot chocolate, Mexican chocolate has a grainier texture than common baking or eating chocolate and contains cinnamon and sometimes almonds. If not available, substitute 1 ounce dark semisweet chocolate, ½ teaspoon ground cinnamon, and a drop of almond extract.

chocolate, white Despite its name, white chocolate is not actually a chocolate since it does not contain cocoa or chocolate liquor. Choose a high-quality white chocolate such as Lindt, Callebaut, or Valrhona. White chocolate does not melt as easily as milk and dark chocolates; as it is stirred, however, it will smooth out.

chorizo, Spanish A coarse pork sausage seasoned with garlic and paprika, Spanish chorizo may be fresh, cured, dried, or smoked, but it always has a slightly tangy flavor. Do not confuse it with Mexican chorizo, which is a spicy fresh sausage.

dulce de leche This canned Latin American dessert sauce is available at specialty-food stores, but it is also easy to make at home: Pour 1 can of condensed milk into a shallow oven-safe dish, cover it with aluminum foil, and bake it in a water bath at 400°F, whisking every 30 minutes, for 1½–2 hours, or until it is caramel in color and has thickened to a nice dipping consistency.

espresso powder, instant Brands like Ferrera and Medaglia D'oro can be found in specialty-food stores. For a substitute, dissolve 1 tablespoon instant coffee in milk or cream before adding it to the other ingredients.

framboise A type of fruit brandy, framboise is a strong, clear spirit distilled from raspberry juice that has been fermented. It is served as an aperitif before or after dinner and is widely used in desserts.

Frangelico An Italian hazelnut liqueur often added to coffee at the end of a meal. Amaretto liqueur can be substituted.

ginger, pickled Familiar to anyone who loves sushi, picked ginger is used in Japan as a palate cleanser. It is available at Asian or specialty-food markets.

grappa Made by distilling grape residuals left over from wine making, grappa is an Italian liqueur that is high in alcohol and is usually enjoyed after dinner.

hoisin sauce This thick, brown, salty-sweet sauce is used as a condiment in Chinese cuisine, and is often referred to as Chinese barbecue sauce. It is made with soybeans, garlic, vinegar, and chiles and is seasoned with spices.

kirsch A cherry-flavored colorless brandy, the best kirsch is made in Germany, France, and Switzerland, where the highly flavorful wild black cherry is used.

kombu This variety of dried sea kelp is a staple of Japanese cuisine. It is usually sold in flakes or small squares that are covered with a salt residue and have a strong taste and fragrance of the sea.

lemongrass Only the pale lower portion of the lemongrass stalk is used. To prepare, cut off and discard the fibrous tops and remove the outer leaves from the base. With the flat side of a broad knife blade, crush the base and then cut as directed in the recipe.

linguiça A mild, cured Portuguese sausage seasoned with vinegar, onions, garlic, and paprika, linguiça is delicious as a fondue dipper when grilled and sliced.

mushrooms, cremini Also known as Italian or Roman mushrooms, or common brown mushrooms, cremini mushrooms mature to become portobellos.

mushrooms, enoki These mushrooms grow in small clumps and have small white caps and slender stems. Their mild flavor and smooth texture make them suitable for use as a garnish for salads, clear soups, and braised dishes.

mushrooms, shiitake Ranging from buff to dark brown in color, fresh shiitake mushrooms have smooth plump caps and sturdy stems that should be trimmed and discarded. The mushrooms are also available dried and are often sold as dried Chinese black mushrooms. The dried mushrooms must be reconstituted in boiling water before use.

napa cabbage Also called Chinese cabbage or celery cabbage, this elongated variety has wrinkly, light yellow-green leaves and a pearly white core.

oil, Asian sesame Unlike clear sesame oil which is made from raw white sesame seeds, Asian sesame oil is dark in color and intense in flavor because it is made with toasted sesame seeds. Use it sparingly as a flavoring.

oil, hot chile This bottled oil, available in Asian markets and many supermarkets, has had hot red chiles steeped in it. It can be refrigerated indefinitely after opening.

peppercorns, Sichuan Not peppercorns, but actually dried berries with a reddish-brown shell, Sichuan peppercorns are milder than black peppercorns and have underlying citrus notes.

rice flour Long-grain rice is ground to produce this flour that is used for making rice noodles and rice paper. It should not be confused with glutinous rice flour, which is made from short-grain glutinous rice and is used for making dumplings and desserts with a chewy consistency.

rice stick noodles Dried rice noodles are labeled "rice sticks" when flat and "rice vermicelli" when round. They can be found at specialty-food stores.

Vietnamese fish sauce (nuoc mam) This salty and pungent seasoning sauce is used throughout Southeast Asia. The amber liquid is the filtered extract of small fish (typically anchovies), salt, and water left to ferment in the sun. The resulting sharp taste mellows with cooking, producing an excellent, rich-tasting dipping sauce.

oyster sauce This concentrated dark brown sauce with a slightly sweet, smoky flavor is made from dried oysters, salt, and water. It has cornstarch and caramel added for consistency and color.

Port True Port comes from the Douro region of Portugal, but similar wines are produced in other parts of the world, like California and Australia. Ruby Port is sweet and strong and usually has a fiery, fruity character. Aged tawny Port has a softer, more mellow flavor and a brownish tinge. Save the more expensive vintage Port for drinking, not cooking.

rice wine, Chinese Rich amber in color with a full-bodied bouquet, Chinese rice wine is the product of fermented glutinous rice and millet that is aged for a minimum of 10 years. It is often used in marinades and sauces. The best quality rice wine is named after the Shaoxing province of China.

sambal oelek This Indonesian chile sauce is made with hot chiles, salt, and sometimes vinegar, and is often used to season Asian soups. It is widely available at grocery stores and specialty-food stores.

sherry, cream A specialty of southwestern Spain, sherry is a fortified wine made from the Palomino Fino grape. It comes in eight different types and is distinguished by color, flavor, sweetness, and alcohol content. Sweet cream sherry is mahogany brown in color and is the sweetest of all the sherries.

squid, preparing You can buy squid cleaned, or to clean yourself, pull the head and tentacles away from the body, or *mantle*, then reach into the mantle and pull out the insides and discard. Rinse out the mantle, then cut off the tentacles above the eyes. Squeeze the cut end of the tentacles to remove the hard "beak" at the base and discard it. Cut the tentacles and mantle as specified in the recipe.

Thai sweet chile sauce This slightly sweet sauce is often used as a dipping sauce or to season a dipping sauce. Brands found in specialty-food stores include Mae Ploy and Mae Pranom.

Triple Sec This liqueur is made by steeping dried orange peel in alcohol. It is often used as a stand in for the more expensive Grand Marnier to flavor cocktails.

udon noodles, dried These wide, white noodles are made from a dough of wheat flour and water. They are sold both dried and fresh and either round or flat.

vinegar, Chinese black This vinegar is made by fermenting a grain (rice, wheat, millet, sorghum) and leaving it to age. They are generally a deep reddish-black color and have a rich, smoky, pleasantly tart taste.

vermouth This fortified wine is available in sweet and red, sweet and white, or dry and white varieties. Dry white vermouth, an ingredient in the classic martini, can also be used in cooking. Substitute it in any recipe calling for dry white wine.

wasabi This root is most often found grated into a paste and served alongside sushi. The powder form, available at specialty-food stores, can be mixed with water to create a paste or sauce.

index

a

Ahi Fondue, Marinated, with Wasabi
Dipping Sauce, 45
Apples, Grilled, 89
Artichokes
Bagna Cauda, 49
Parmesan and Artichoke Dip
Fondue, 20

b

Bacon
Edam Fondue with Bacon and
Smothered Onions, 18
Southwestern Layered Fondue, 31
Bagna Cauda, 49
Baked Pita Strips, 88
Beef
Beef Fondue with Creamy
Horseradish Sauce, 53
Beef Stock, 97
Shabu-Shabu, 62
thin-slicing, 99
Vietnamese Beef and Vinegar
Hot Pot, 61
Bell peppers
cutting into squares, 102
Mongolian Hot Pot, 60
Romesco Sauce, 94
Bittersweet Chocolate Fondue, 73
Blue Cheese Fondue with Port-
Glazed Shallots, 23
Bok choy
Mongolian Hot Pot, 60
Sichuan Hot Pot, 59
Bourbon-Caramel Fondue, 74
Bread, cutting into cubes, 98
Brie Fondue with Mushrooms and
Herbs, 32
Broth fondues
basics of, 56–57
Chicken Fondue with Romesco
Sauce, 65

Mongolian Hot Pot, 60
Shabu-Shabu, 62
Sichuan Hot Pot, 59
Thai Curry Hot Pot with Seafood, 66
Vietnamese Beef and Vinegar
Hot Pot, 61

c

Cabbage
Mongolian Hot Pot, 60
Shabu-Shabu, 62
Sichuan Hot Pot, 59
Thai Curry Hot Pot with
Seafood, 66
Caramel Corn Clusters, 91
Caramelized Shallot Halves, 89
Cheese fondues
basics of, 10–11
Blue Cheese Fondue with Port-
Glazed Shallots, 23
Brie Fondue with Mushrooms
and Herbs, 32
Cheddar and Ale Fondue, 35
Chile-Spiced Chèvre and Brown
Sugar Fondue, 83
Classic Swiss Fondue, 13
Cream Cheese and Crabmeat
Fondue, 25
Edam Fondue with Bacon and
Smothered Onions, 18
Fontina Fondue with Truffle Oil, 17
French Onion Soup Fondue, 30
Manchego Fondue with Piquillo
Peppers and Toasted Garlic, 26
Mascarpone–Vanilla Bean
Fondue, 78
Normandy-Style Fondue, 24
Parmesan and Artichoke Dip
Fondue, 20
Pepper Jack Fondue with
Roasted Garlic, 19

Provolone Fondue with Sun-Dried
Tomato Pesto, 36
Queso Fundido, 14
Smoked Salmon Fondue with
Cream Cheese and Dill, 29
Southwestern Layered Fondue, 31
Chèvre, Chile-Spiced, and Brown
Sugar Fondue, 83
Chicken
Chicken Fondue with Romesco
Sauce, 65
Chicken Fondue with Spicy
Peanut Sauce, 44
Chicken Stock, 96–97
Sichuan Hot Pot, 59
Chiles
Chile-Spiced Chèvre and Brown
Sugar Fondue, 83
Chipotle Tartar Sauce, 95
Pineapple-Chile Salsa, 93
Queso Fundido, 14
Chocolate
Bittersweet Chocolate Fondue, 73
chopping, 103
Mexican Chocolate Fondue with
Orange Essence, 80
Peanut Butter and Chocolate
Fondue, 85
Swiss-Style Chocolate Fondue, 79
Churros, 90–91
Cinnamon-Sugar Tortilla Chips, 88
Classic Swiss Fondue, 13
Coconut and coconut milk
Thai Curry Hot Pot with Seafood, 66
Toasted Coconut and White
Chocolate Fondue with Rum, 77
Corn
Caramel Corn Clusters, 91
Southwestern Layered Fondue, 31
Cream Cheese and Crabmeat
Fondue, 25

Cream cheese
    Cream Cheese and Crabmeat
        Fondue, 25
    Parmesan and Artichoke Dip
        Fondue, 20
    Smoked Salmon Fondue with
        Cream Cheese and Dill, 29
Creamy Horseradish Sauce, 94–95
Crêpes, Sweet, 91

d

Dessert fondues
    basics of, 70–71
    Bittersweet Chocolate Fondue, 73
    Bourbon-Caramel Fondue, 74
    Chile-Spiced Chèvre and Brown
        Sugar Fondue, 83
    Dulce de Leche Fondue, 84
    Mascarpone–Vanilla Bean
        Fondue, 78
    Mexican Chocolate Fondue with
        Orange Essence, 80
    Peanut Butter and Chocolate
        Fondue, 85
    Swiss-Style Chocolate Fondue, 79
    Toasted Coconut and White
        Chocolate Fondue with Rum, 77
    White Chocolate–Espresso
        Fondue, 86
Dippers, homemade
    Baked Pita Strips, 88
    Caramel Corn Clusters, 91
    Caramelized Shallot Halves, 89
    Churros, 90–91
    Cinnamon-Sugar Tortilla Chips, 88
    Grilled Apples, 89
    Polenta Cubes, 88–89
    Sugar Twists, 89–90
    Sweet Crêpes, 91
    Tortilla Chips, 88
Dulce de Leche Fondue, 84

e

Edam Fondue with Bacon and
    Smothered Onions, 18

Emmentaler cheese
    Classic Swiss Fondue, 13
    Parmesan and Artichoke Dip
        Fondue, 20

f

Fennel, cutting, 103
Firepots. See Broth fondues
Fish
    Marinated Ahi Fondue with
        Wasabi Dipping Sauce, 45
    Smoked Salmon Fondue with
        Cream Cheese and Dill, 29
    Swordfish Fondue with Lemon-
        Caper Rémoulade, 51
    Thai Curry Hot Pot with Seafood, 66
Fontina Fondue with Truffle Oil, 17
French Onion Soup Fondue, 30

g

Garlic
    Garlic-Soy Dipping Sauce, 96
    Pepper Jack Fondue with Roasted
        Garlic, 19
Grilled Apples, 89
Gruyère cheese
    Classic Swiss Fondue, 13
    French Onion Soup Fondue, 30

h

Havarti cheese
    Blue Cheese Fondue with Port-
        Glazed Shallots, 23
    Brie Fondue with Mushrooms
        and Herbs, 32
    Normandy-Style Fondue, 24
Herbed Ponzu Dipping Sauce, 96
Honey-Mustard Sauce, 94
Horseradish Sauce, Creamy, 94–95
Hot pots. See Broth fondues

l

Lamb
    Mongolian Hot Pot, 60
Lemon-Caper Rémoulade, 95

m

Manchego Fondue with Piquillo
    Peppers and Toasted Garlic, 26
Mango Relish, 92–93
Marinated Ahi Fondue with Wasabi
    Dipping Sauce, 45
Mascarpone–Vanilla Bean Fondue, 78
Mexican Chocolate Fondue with
    Orange Essence, 80
Mongolian Hot Pot, 60
Monterey jack cheese
    Edam Fondue with Bacon and
        Smothered Onions, 18
    Manchego Fondue with Piquillo
        Peppers and Toasted Garlic, 26
    Normandy-Style Fondue, 24
    Queso Fundido, 14
Mushrooms
    Brie Fondue with Mushrooms
        and Herbs, 32
    Mongolian Hot Pot, 60
    Mushroom-Herb Paste, 92
    Shabu-Shabu, 62
    Sichuan Hot Pot, 59
    Thai Curry Hot Pot with Seafood, 66

n

Noodles
    Mongolian Hot Pot, 60
    Shabu-Shabu, 62
    Sichuan Hot Pot, 59
    Thai Curry Hot Pot with Seafood, 66
Normandy-Style Fondue, 24

o

Oil fondues
    basics of, 40–41
    Bagna Cauda, 49
    Beef Fondue with Creamy
        Horseradish Sauce, 53
    Chicken Fondue with Spicy
        Peanut Sauce, 44
    Marinated Ahi Fondue with
        Wasabi Dipping Sauce, 45

Pork Fondue with Mango Relish, 46
Sausage and Potato Fondue with
    Honey-Mustard Sauce, 50
Shrimp and Scallop Fondue with
    Chipotle Tartar Sauce, 43
Swordfish Fondue with Lemon-
    Caper Rémoulade, 51
Onions
    Edam Fondue with Bacon and
        Smothered Onions, 18
    French Onion Soup Fondue, 30
    Pickled Onions, 92

p

Parmesan and Artichoke Dip Fondue,
    20
Peanut butter
    Peanut Butter and Chocolate
        Fondue, 85
    Spicy Peanut Sauce, 93–94
Pepper Jack Fondue with Roasted
    Garlic, 19
Pickled Onions, 92
Pineapple
    cubing, 103
    Pineapple-Chile Salsa, 93
Pita Strips, Baked, 88
Polenta Cubes, 88–89
Pork
    Pork Fondue with Mango Relish, 46
    Sichuan Hot Pot, 59
Potatoes
    cooking and cutting up, 101
    Sausage and Potato Fondue with
        Honey-Mustard Sauce, 50
Pots
    for broth fondues, 56
    for cheese fondues, 10
    for dessert fondues, 70
    for oil fondues, 40
Provolone Fondue with Sun-Dried
    Tomato Pesto, 36

q

Queso Fundido, 14

r

Relish, Mango, 92–93
Romesco Sauce, 94

s

Salmon Fondue, Smoked, with
    Cream Cheese and Dill, 29
Sauces and salsas
    Chipotle Tartar Sauce, 95
    Creamy Horseradish Sauce, 94–95
    Garlic-Soy Dipping Sauce, 96
    Herbed Ponzu Dipping Sauce, 96
    Honey-Mustard Sauce, 94
    Lemon-Caper Rémoulade, 95
    Mango Relish, 92–93
    Pineapple-Chile Salsa, 93
    Romesco Sauce, 94
    Sesame-Soy Dipping Sauce, 96
    Spicy Peanut Sauce, 93–94
    Wasabi Dipping Sauce, 95–96
Sausage
    Queso Fundido, 14
    Sausage and Potato Fondue with
        Honey-Mustard Sauce, 50
Scallop and Shrimp Fondue with
    Chipotle Tartar Sauce, 43
Sesame-Soy Dipping Sauce, 96
Shabu-Shabu, 62
Shallot Halves, Caramelized, 89
Shrimp
    Shrimp and Scallop Fondue with
        Chipotle Tartar Sauce, 43
    Thai Curry Hot Pot with Seafood, 66
Sichuan Hot Pot, 59
Smoked Salmon Fondue with Cream
    Cheese and Dill, 29
Southwestern Layered Fondue, 31
Spicy Peanut Sauce, 93–94
Squid
    Thai Curry Hot Pot with Seafood, 66
Steamboat pots. See Broth fondues
Stocks
    Beef Stock, 97
    Chicken Stock, 96–97
Sugar Twists, 89–90

Sweet Crêpes, 91
Swiss-Style Chocolate Fondue, 79
Swiss Fondue, Classic, 13
Swordfish Fondue with Lemon-Caper
    Rémoulade, 51

t

Tartar Sauce, Chipotle, 95
Thai Curry Hot Pot with Seafood, 66
Toasted Coconut and White
    Chocolate Fondue with Rum, 77
Tofu
    Mongolian Hot Pot, 60
    Shabu-Shabu, 62
    Sichuan Hot Pot, 59

v

Vegetables. See also individual
    vegetables
    Bagna Cauda, 49
    blanching, 100
    Sichuan Hot Pot, 59
    Vietnamese Beef and Vinegar
        Hot Pot, 61

w

Wasabi Dipping Sauce, 95–96
White chocolate
    Toasted Coconut and White
        Chocolate Fondue with Rum, 77
    White Chocolate–Espresso Fondue, 86

FONDUE

A WELDON OWEN PRODUCTION
1045 Sansome Street, Suite 100
San Francisco, CA 94111
www.weldonowen.com

Printed and bound by 1010 in China
First printed in 2018
10 9 8 7 6 5 4 3 2 1

Library of Congress Cataloging-in-Publication
data is available.

ISBN: 978-1-68188-430-1

WELDON OWEN, INC.
President & Publisher Roger Shaw
SVP, Sales & Marketing Amy Kaneko
Finance & Operations Director Thomas Morgan

Associate Publisher Amy Marr
Senior Editor Lisa Atwood

Creative Director Kelly Booth
Art Director Marisa Kwek
Production Designer Howie Severson

Production Director Michelle Duggan
Production Manager Sam Bissell
Imaging Manager Don Hill

Photographer Alex Farnum
Food Stylist Shelly Kaldunski

Weldon Owen is a division of Bonnier Publishing USA
www.bonnierpublishingusa.com

ACKNOWLEDGMENTS

Weldon Owen wishes to thank the following people for their generous support in producing this book:
Prop Stylist Daniele Maxwell; **Photographer's Assistant** Daniel Baker; **Food Stylist's Assistant** Ara Armstrong;
Editorial Consultant Dawn Yanagihara; **Recipe Consultant** Shelly Kaldunski; **Copyeditors** Heather Belt and Sharon Silva;
Proofreader Kathryn Shedrick; and **Indexer** Ken DellaPenta. Thanks also to Gaye Allen, Kara Church, Lauren Hancock,
Julia Humes, Ashley Martinez, Delbarr Navai, Jennifer Newens, and Hannah Rahill,

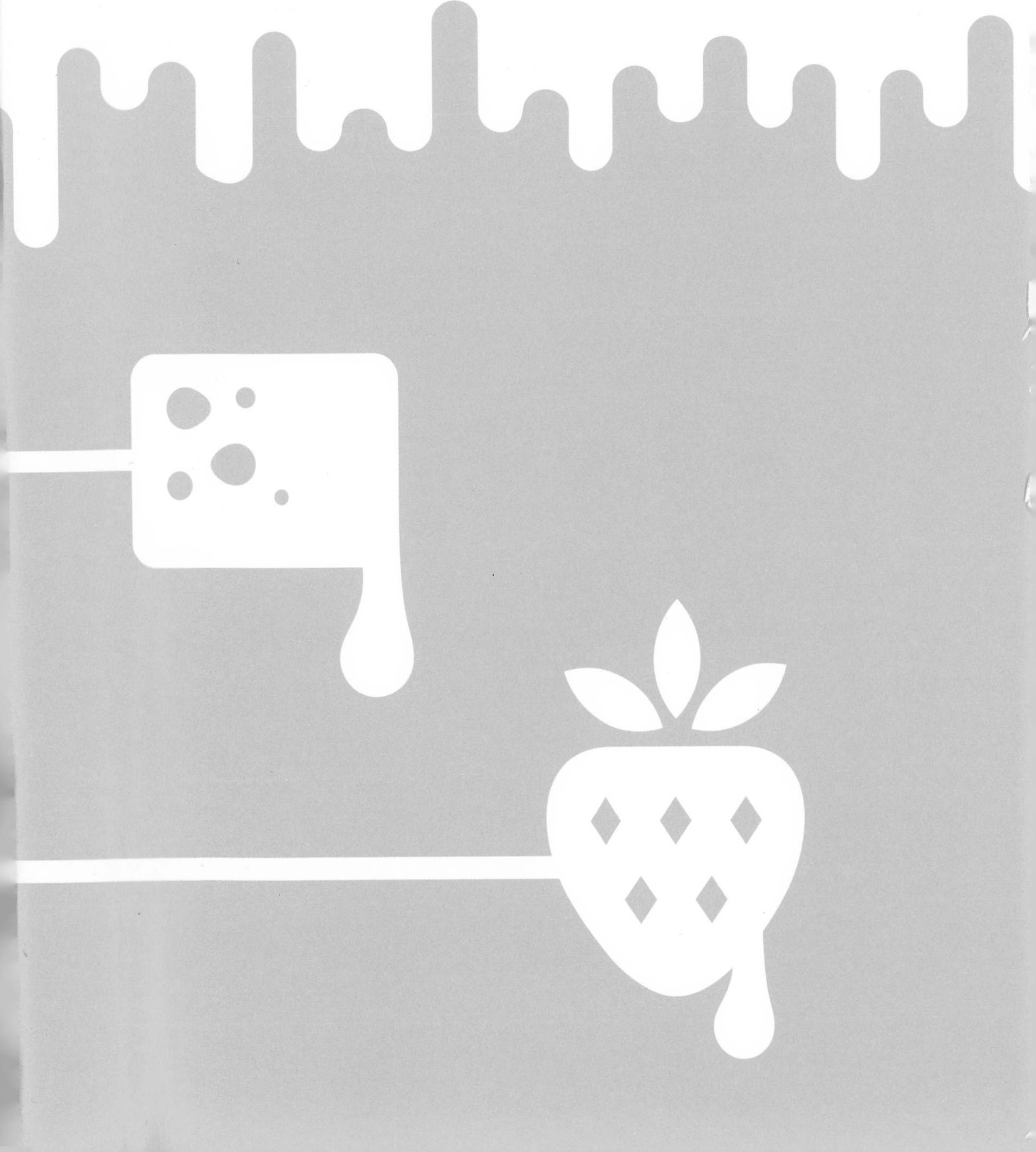